Donald C. Posterski

REINVENTING Evangelism

NEW
STRATEGIES
FOR PRESENTING
CHRIST
IN TODAY'S
WORLD

INTERVARSITY PRESS
DOWNERS GROVE, ILLINOIS, U.S.A.
MARKHAM, ONTARIO, CANADA

InterVarsity Press
P.O. Box 1400, Downers Grove, Illinois 60515, U.S.A.
860 Denison St., Unit 3, Markham, Ontario L3R 4H1, Canada

© 1989 by Donald C. Posterski

All rights reserved. No part of this publication may be reproduced, stored in a retrieval system or transmitted in any form or by any means, electronic, mechanical, photocopying, recording or otherwise, without the prior permission of InterVarsity Press.

InterVarsity Press, U.S.A., is the book-publishing division of InterVarsity Christian Fellowship, U.S.A., a student movement active on campus at hundreds of universities, colleges and schools of nursing. For information about local and regional activities, write Public Relations Dept., InterVarsity Christian Fellowship, 6400 Schroeder Rd., P.O. Box 7895, Madison, WI 53707-7895.

InterVarsity Press, Canada, is the literature division of Inter-Varsity Christian Fellowship of Canada, which is a movement of students active in high schools, schools of nursing, colleges and universities, and of adults active in youth programs at Pioneer Camps. For information about these ministries, write Inter-Varsity Christian Fellowship, 1840 Lawrence Ave. E., Scarborough, Ontario M1R 2Y4.

InterVarsity Christian Fellowship, U.S.A., and Inter-Varsity Christian Fellowship of Canada are charter members of the International Fellowship of Evangelical Students.

All Scripture quotations, unless otherwise indicated, are from the Holy Bible, New International Version. Copyright © 1973, 1978, International Bible Society. Used by permission of Zondervan Bible Publishers.

Cover photograph: Michael Goss

USA ISBN 0-8308-1269-5
CAN ISBN 0-88918-002-4
Printed in the United States of America ∞

Library of Congress Cataloging-in-Publication Data

Posterski, Donald C., 1942-
  Reinventing evangelism.

  Bibliography: p.
  Includes index.
  1. Evangelistic work.   I. Title.
BV3790.P652   1989   269'.2   89-15363
ISBN 0-8308-1269-5

Canadian Cataloguing in Publication Data

  Posterski, Donald C., 1942-
    Reinventing evangelism

  ISBN 0-88918-002-4 (Can. ed.)
  ISBN 0-8308-1269-5 (U.S. ed.)

  1. Evangelistic work.   I. Title.

  BV3790.P68 1989   253.7   C89-094610-8

| 17 | 16 | 15 | 14 | 13 | 12 | 11 | 10 | 9 | 8 | 7 | 6 | 5 | 4 | 3 | 2 | 1 |
| 99 | 98 | 97 | 96 | 95 | 94 | 93 | 92 | 91 | 90 | 89 | | | | | | |

To Mom and Dad . . . Jean and Frank
For pointing me in so many right directions.

Preface

Why write another book on evangelism? Aren't our bookshelves already overloaded with admonitions on the subject? I readily admit the risk to make yet another statement on the church's commitment to invite the world to respond to the claims of Christ. However, when the culture is shifting and the world is winning, we need to re-examine our assumptions about evangelism and be certain our approaches are connecting with the times.

This book has been written with the Bible in one hand and computer printouts in the other. As a self-confessed "culture watcher," I've repeatedly walked into the world with a video camera to capture what was going on "out there" and then retreated to make a biblical response. Sometimes, wide-angle shots brought general social trends into focus. On other occasions, close-ups spotlighted more specific circumstances in today's secularizing society. The aim was always to project implications for evangelism in these modern times. The intent was to equip Christians to relate appropriately and offer a credible gospel to the people in their natural networks who have come to non-Christian conclusions about life.

In the past few years, my inner spirit has often been prodded by the good examples of fine people who have no evident regard for God. They have disrupted some of my Christian assumptions and driven me to a deeper honesty about life. This journey has not always been pleasant, or for that matter, inspiring to my personal faith. I'm convinced that many who call themselves committed Christians have a lot to learn from the people in their lives they identify as non-Christians.

One of the creative surprises God brought into my life was connecting me with my research colleague Reg Bibby. For the past six years our lives have repeatedly intersected. I'm grateful for our friendship and his expertise. I am also indebted to the people who graciously pre-read this manuscript. Jim Berney, Pete Hammond, Jean Nordlund, Marty Bell, Glenn Smith, Gordon Aeschliman and my wife, Beth, will all recognize their points of influence in the final text. Friends John McLaverty and Gary Nelson have not only provided a regular luncheon forum to discuss my ideas and personal concerns—their probings kept me accountable on a wide range of life's issues. John Wilkinson's sustained interest in the progress of the project was especially encouraging. Canadian InterVarsity's gift of a sabbatical leave gave me time to think as well as to write. I remain grateful for the people who believed enough in me and the venture to offer their input.

There is a looming crisis on the horizon for the Christian church in North America. Research presses the conclusion that there are few differences between the people in our society who regularly go to church when compared to those who do their laundry or go golfing on Sunday morning. The consequences are severe. Non-Christians perceive that Christianity makes no qualitative difference to life on this earth and conclude, "Why bother?" Christians seem to have little to offer beyond the invitation to a privatized faith experience and some new social contacts. *Reinventing Evangelism* is written with this indicting dilemma in mind.

In the past, North American culture has been decidedly pro-Christian. In the present, many sectors of the society are simply passive toward the faith. "If you prefer that brand of belief for yourself, that's fine with me" is the attitude. In the future, we can expect increasing anti-Christian sentiment toward the claims of Christ and toward the people who hold firmly to the Lord's views. Followers of Jesus who understand the dynamics of what is happening around them will be more prepared than surprised.

Donald C. Posterski

Introduction

My friend Chuck lives on the outskirts of San Diego. His back yard extends out into a canyonlike gorge. A series of towering electrical power poles linked together with high-tension wires wind their way down the gorge carrying electricity into the city.

Late one evening Chuck was in his living room when he heard an explosion. In the same moment the lights in his home flickered and then went out. The loud sound came from the gorge. Chuck rushed to his back yard. The source of the problem was readily evident— there was a fire blazing near the top of one of the power poles.

The reason for the problem was a matter of greater concern. As the fire died down and the smoke drifted away, the form of a human body could be seen draped over the extended arm of the pole.

The disaster was another of those unnecessary human horror stories. A group of young people were having a party together. After having too much to drink, a twenty-year-old who was also an avid mountain climber decided to demonstrate his skills for the crowd. It was his last climb.

The incident made front-page news the next morning. For most, the event was just another item that got discarded with the pile of old newspapers. Some weeks later as Chuck reflected on the tragedy, sorrow was still in his spirit as he mused, "That young man was somebody's son. It was such a meaningless death."

Making the Meaningless Meaningful

There is another death that is being robbed of its meaning. The crucifixion of Jesus Christ still makes the news with regularity, but the significance of his death is laced with distortion. Jesus continues to parade with prominence in the culture, but his reputation is repeatedly marred and scarred. High-profile leaders sometimes give him bad press. Many of his followers start with enthusiasm, but in the end, their joy ebbs away and they betray him.

How do we make the gospel heard? How do we make the gospel news again in a society that habitually celebrates Christmas and sings carols in Jesus' honor without ever pausing to ponder the religious implications of the advent?

Restoring Jesus to the true status he deserves will not be an easy task. Making more announcements about Jesus will do little to nudge North Americans toward genuine personal faith in him. Religious holidays will remind us of Jesus' life, but for most people the greater gift will be the day off work that the holiday bestows. The usual pages of church advertisements in the country's newspapers inviting everyone to attend the Christmas or Easter Sunday services won't really make much difference.

Our old strategies to reach others with the gospel, for the most part, simply no longer work. This book develops this theme in detail, but for now we may simply observe that our culture is rapidly losing its Christian foundations. We can't assume people understand what we mean by "salvation," "sin," "heaven," "good and evil" or even "God" when we talk about our faith. And just as Jesus understood the culture he was trying to reach and tailored his message to it, so too we must understand our times and adjust our strategies accordingly. It is time to reinvent our evangelism.

In today's world, reinventing our evangelism means that we must go beyond words. Our society desperately needs serious followers of Jesus who will engage the culture with a coherent gospel. Engaging the culture in order to present a credible gospel will require clear choices and deliberate strategies from today's Christians.

We need to become Christian *meaning-makers*. Meaning-makers are people who make sense of life, people who make sense of God, people whose lives ring with clarity in the midst of contemporary ambiguity, people who have integrity, people who reside in today's world revealing with their living and their lips that Jesus' death is the source of vital life.

In the following chapters we will explore what it is like to be Christians in today's world, we will see how we can become meaning-makers for our neighbors, and we will develop new perspectives and strategies for engaging our culture with the gospel.

Chapter One

LEAVING OUR SAFETY ZONES

R ECENTLY, I RECEIVED A LONG LETTER FROM A FRIEND and former student named Linda that spells out some of the challenges of being loyal to Jesus in today's world. She writes: I've come up against a problem that I thought you could help me out with. I'm finding that my life in the work world is very different from what life was like as a student. In school you have the choice of who to hang around with. In an office setting, the choices are limited unless you want to alienate yourself from the people around you, but I don't think that is what Christ wants.

I'm finding that being a Christian in this setting is very difficult and very confusing. What I'm finding more and more as I speak with people is that we Christians are the minority, and their way of life is the norm. I know that by living a Christian lifestyle, one reveals a difference. I also know that when opportunities arise, it is necessary to challenge what people are advocating—though without judging the person. Sometimes I am successful and sometimes I fail. But I'm realizing that in this day and age it is next to impossible to really challenge their views.

The people in my office aren't killers or perverts. They are likable, warm and considerate people. They are people who are trying to find happiness wherever they can. I can name four people that I work with every day who live with their girlfriend or boyfriend. I am especially close to Fran, who is one of the nicest people I've met in a long time, yet she lives with her boyfriend and has fooled around on him. Occasionally, the weekends include drugs for her.

You know the old saying, "Love the sinner; hate the sin." But what do you say to someone who doesn't believe they are sinning? How do I live in this world and not be of this world? There's only so much you can do. What is my alternative? To retreat into an isolated Christian existence and just relate to other Christians, who, like me, are trying to work out their relationship with Christ? Or do I use my office situation as a base to build from and continue my struggle with the world?

I feel caught between two worlds. I'm forced to play the game of life with two different sets of rules. I follow one set while everyone around me follows another!

Linda is facing what all of us face: How can we be ambassadors for Christ in a world that doesn't speak our language? How can we bring Christ to a generation that seems to be running from him at a record-breaking pace? This book addresses this modern-day evangelistic dilemma.

Today Is Not Like Yesterday

In these times it can seem as if God is losing and Satan is winning in the world. The strong Christian consensus from the past is crumbling. In the old days, we lived with assumptions. We did not argue about the rightness of sex being reserved for a marriage relationship. Certainly many people were experimenting with sex outside of marriage, but there was a social consensus that it was wrong. Today, sexual expression is considered to be a matter of personal preference. The waiver of yesterday's stigma is a sign of the times. Those of us who hold to previous standards are affected by what is new around us. We begin to wonder about what is really nonnegotiable.

The definition of a family, for instance, can no longer be taken for granted. Until recently a family was understood to mean a married man and woman living together with one or more sons or daughters. The increasing number of single parents is changing the family paradigm. Young mothers having babies outside of marriage and choosing to raise their children on their own is introducing social complexity. Divorce can usher in a variety of changes in family structures as children share time with parents in different households, welcome new stepsiblings and sometimes a new stepparent. Common-law relationships, and homosexual partners desiring to be parents, extend the definition of a family in this age. The existence of sperm banks and the practice of surrogate-mother births have taken us where we have not been before.

A new force affecting society today is feminism. Christians find themselves having to think clearly and make major adjustments. A number of churches are debating the issue of the ordination of women. Some religious traditions continue to follow the practice of not letting women preach and teach. For Christians, historical teaching about the husband being the "head of the home" frequently got mistranslated to mean that "Dad wasn't supposed to peel potatoes in the kitchen." The predictability of male-female roles has been dismantled. Change is disruptive; social shifts have a price tag.

Another shift in the culture that has caught many off guard revolves around authority and obedience—which used to be stabilizing forces in society. Today, the dynamics in life that allowed institutions and people with position to speak with authority have disintegrated.

The church is an example. In the past, church leaders from all traditions spoke authoritatively in the realm of ethics and morals. The Bible was an accepted reference point of appeal, both for those who followed it and those who didn't. In the family, the father was the historical authority figure, and children obeyed him without question. Similarly, principals of schools were automatically respected because of their positions. The same deference was paid to politicians and teachers.

Author and management consultant Peter Drucker aptly reminds us that we are struggling with "the erosion of continuities." Many stable reference points from the past have been worn away. Serious Christians can't help but wonder where to take a stand. We feel pushed around by the new norms.

Sociologist Peter Berger contends that our culture no longer has generally acknowledged "plausibility structures."[1] His point is that in our contemporary society we live without structures that can be taken for granted without argument. In practice, what used to be considered deviant behaviors are now acceptable options in the range of "normal" lifestyle choices. A "pluralistic society" is the coinage we use to describe our present status. This reality is challenging the confidence of some of God's most faithful people. Certainly, today is not like yesterday, and there are serious consequences for Christians.

Where Are the Differences?

It is getting harder to distinguish the Christians from the non-Christians. Charles Colson observes that "we live in a time that would seem to be marked by unprecedented spiritual resurgence: 96 percent of all Americans say they believe in God; 80 percent profess to be Christians. . . . 50 million Americans claim to be born again. Yet families are splitting apart in record numbers. There are 100 times more burglaries in so-called 'Christian' America than in so-called 'pagan' Japan. Why this paradox between profession and practice?" Colson wonders. "Why is the faith of so many not making an impact on the moral values of our land?"[2]

Researchers and other noted authorities are beginning to probe a sensitive area for modern Christians. They are raising sobering questions about whether those who make belief claims and attend church are behaving any differently from those who do not. After years of accumulating research from various sources, George Gallup, Jr., states: "Church attendance, it appears, makes little difference in people's ethical views and behavior with respect to lying, cheating, pilferage, and not reporting theft."[3]

Dean Borgman, professor and youth ministry expert, recently wrote, "The gap between the mores of Christian and church kids and those of the general culture is much narrower than ever before. Your kids are more into materialism and relativism of the world and more of them are indulging in sex and drug highs than you think."[4]

In his precedent-setting book *Fragmented Gods,* sociologist Reginald Bibby concludes, "Religion in Canada shows little sign of having either a unique voice or a unique influence. Canadians who are religiously committed construct reality in much the same manner as others. They relate with neither more nor less compassion. They experience a level of well-being that is neither higher nor lower than other people's."[5] Indeed, it can be hard to find a qualitative difference between lifestyles of Christians and others.

A working mother in her early thirties, Angela was back into the dating game following her divorce. She was also a committed Christian and intent on putting her faith into practice—including her sexual lifestyle. In recent months, Angela had gone out with several men who also went to her church. Being the mother of a young son, she was not naive about life, but she was surprised by her dates' bold sexual advances.

After a Sunday morning worship service, Angela cornered two of her single female friends in the church lobby to get an update on

Christian dating expectations. Angela discreetly sketched her experience and candidly asked, "The message I'm getting is that after two or three dates, expecting to have sex is part of the package. Am I reading it right?" Her two friends exchanged glances and after an awkward moment, one of them responded, "That's about it." The other person simply nodded in agreement.

Although there is insufficient hard data to be definitive, there is enough evidence to wonder and worry about whether the church has been captured by the culture. Like Linda who was negotiating her transition into the work world, Christians are struggling with how to relate to the world around them. How can we avoid being "of" the world when we are so deeply "in" it?

Jesus and Zacchaeus

There is a wonderful story in Luke 19:1-10 about Jesus' interactions with an undesirable tax collector named Zacchaeus. By watching how Jesus interacted with the world, perhaps we can find some lessons for our own lives.

According to the account, Jesus is on his way toward Jerusalem and is just "passing through" Jericho (v. 1). Zacchaeus, the chief tax collector and a notable citizen of Jericho, has obviously heard about Jesus beforehand. There is some probability that Zacchaeus was an acquaintance of Levi—another tax collector, but one who had become a follower of Jesus. And it could be that Levi had talked to Jesus about Zacchaeus. Whatever the background of this profound encounter, Zacchaeus positions himself part way up a sycamore-fig tree to be sure he has a clear view of Jesus (v. 4). Zacchaeus knew that climbing trees does not enhance one's social standing, but his curiosity must have been stronger than his immediate concern for his reputation.

The Scriptures do not give a complete account of the incident, but the next move is from Jesus. He sees Zacchaeus and immediately perceives the extraordinary interest. In Jesus' mind, bold initiative that prompts a person to climb a tree deserved unusual initiative in return.

He gives his full attention to Zacchaeus and, with the crowd listening to every word, Jesus closes the distance between the two of them: "Zacchaeus, come down immediately. I must stay at your house today" (v. 5).

Jesus was immediately criticized, not for his forward social behavior, but rather for his blatant association with a prominent sinner (v. 7). Zacchaeus was a "publican" which in the eyes of religious Jews made him a member of the despised class of humanity. Among the Jews it was unheard of for a rabbi to pollute himself by spending time in a house with such a person. Onlookers in the crowd were offended that Jesus would even allow himself to be entertained by Zacchaeus.[6]

But Jesus was more attentive to Zacchaeus's interests than he was to the concern of his critics. He knew that if anything of spiritual significance was to happen, he and Zacchaeus would need uninterrupted private time. Jesus also understood that in order for their time to be really fruitful, it would be important to be where Zacchaeus was most at ease. Consequently, Jesus left his safety zone and entered Zacchaeus's comfort zone. In Jesus' mind, spending the evening in Zacchaeus's home was the ideal place to be.

The contrast between Zacchaeus and Jesus was staggering. Zacchaeus was wealthy. Jesus was poor. Zacchaeus was a specialist at calculating what to take from other people. Jesus was a specialist at giving things away. We do not know all that took place at Zacchaeus's home, but we can imagine the fine food, the laughter, the discussion and interaction.

At one point Zacchaeus looked across the table at Jesus and made a decision. Without any hint of wanting to negotiate the terms, he stood up from the table and announced: "Look, Lord! Here and now I give half of my possessions to the poor, and if I have cheated anybody out of anything, I will pay back four times the amount" (v. 8).

The conversation over the dinner table with Jesus did more than just reorder Zacchaeus's thinking. His heart was touched. Greed was converted into generosity. Past dishonesty was countered with restitution. Zacchaeus's encounter with Jesus inspired behavioral change. He became a different person.

Jesus was quick to endorse Zacchaeus's declaration of newfound faith: "Today salvation has come to this house, because this man, too, is a son of Abraham. For the Son of Man came to seek and to save what was lost" (vv. 9-10).

When salvation comes, and the Spirit of God breaks into the human spirit, the consequences are profound. There are many reasons to celebrate. George MacDonald describes what happened to Zacchaeus that night and reminds us of the radical changes that transpire when we encounter Christ. He asks:

> What is salvation? To be delivered from everything mean, low, despicable, selfish, cringing, fearing in my whole nature, that I may stand humble yet bold and free before the Universe of God, because God knows me, and I know God. That is salvation.[7]

Decaffeinated Christianity

Speaking with reference to the Christian populace in the United States, Anglican Bishop Michael Marshall suggests that "the problem with contemporary Christianity in America is that many people have settled for a facsimile of Christian freedom: running their own lives while at the same time saying they believe in Christ." He further contends that many so-called believers have accepted a "decaffeinated Christianity—it promises not to keep you awake at night."[8] If the bishop's analysis is accurate, we should not be surprised that the faith claims of so many are having so little impact on modern society.

The present state of affairs introduces critical consequences for evangelism. A brand of belief that doesn't prompt the loss of sleep in our troubled and needy world will not wake others up to their need to be redeemed in Christ. What incentive is there to investigate a faith that has lost its reputation for making a difference? If the modern brand of Christianity is not producing behavioral change, in all honesty, what do Christians have to offer to those who are not Christians?

When Zacchaeus staked out his spot to get a clear view of Jesus, in the back of his mind he had a hunch that what Jesus had to offer was more than Zacchaeus already possessed. The longer he and Jesus spent together, the more he became convinced that what Jesus stood for was worth his allegiance. Before the night ended, Zacchaeus made his move toward the forgiveness of God, and his life was reordered. He was transformed. During the next week Zacchaeus's behavior was the talk of the town. And word got around that God was the reason for it all.

Unless word gets around about the behavior of the people who verbally claim belief in God, those who do not believe will have little interest in those claims—or in anything deeper with God.

Generosity Makes News

Zacchaeus's generosity made news. It still does today, especially in a world where the drive to *get* is far more powerful than the desire to *give*.

A few months ago, I received a surprise letter from Maurice along with a crisp, new, twenty-dollar bill. The money turned out to be a deliberate double payment for a book. Maurice had ended up at an event without his wallet, and had arranged to take the book with him and pay later. The letter included a thank-you for trusting him and the following stimulating statement: "Enclosed is $20. I add the extra amount in case, at some future date, your trust may be misplaced, and some deadbeat will forget to pay you, in which case you will be prepaid." Maurice is living like a follower of Jesus. He is practicing generosity and adding a touch of creativity to make life a more beautiful affair.

I have a friend who loves God, works hard, makes lots of money and gives an inordinate amount of what he makes to many causes. One day over lunch, in a quiet way, he was telling me about an experience with one of his non-Christian business partners. The two of them had just gone through a difficult year. A major venture had failed and the financial losses were large. Their relationship was stressed and stretched.

"I did what I could to be honorable through all the proceedings," he shared. "I was still surprised when my partner gave me a gift for Christmas. It was a book. The content of the book is not what is important to me. But what he inscribed is what I value. I flipped open the cover and read: 'To the only person I know who gives more than he takes.' "

In a world gripped by greed, generosity is beautiful. It is like the sun breaking though the clouds on a dismal rainy day. Generosity breeds generosity. Whether the gift is money, time, thoughtfulness, a bouquet of flowers, a special candlelit meal, a crafted word sent on a piece of plain paper or on an elaborate card—generosity lifts the level of life to what God intends for his creation. In this age when there is ambiguity about how Christians are different from those who have come to other conclusions about life, a lifestyle characterized by generosity speaks out for God and lifts up Jesus.

Who Is My Neighbor?

Jesus went to Zacchaeus's home. Can we do the same with our non-Christian neighbors? The sad fact is that many serious Christians have few significant relationships with non-Christians. Do we even know our neighbors? We have always thought of neighbors as the people who live next door. What about the people we work with? Commute with? Jog with?

As a lawyer, Steven built his significant relationships among his legal colleagues. The major focus of his life revolved around his profession. He was known in the courthouse as "Steve." He had more natural neighbor contact at his office than he had where he slept at night. Like many of us, Steve's workplace was the setting for his most primary relationships.

Our social patterns are shifting. Life is revolving around work, school, the immediate family, leisure choices, shared interests and also geographical neighborhoods. As a result, restricting "our neighbors" to people who live close by is inadequate. We will better understand Jesus' command to love our neighbors (Lk 10:25-29) when we see that *our neighbors are the people who normally intersect our lives in the natural flow of our days and nights.*

Accordingly, when we chart the activity patterns of our days and nights and name the people in our natural networks, we define the focus of our mission in this world. These are the people we are to love. When we draw the circumference of our lives around our work and leisure world, around where we live and what we do—we identify the places and the people where God wants to help us make Christ known.

"Of" But Not "In"

One afternoon, I asked my former pastor why he looked so discouraged. He immediately admitted his low emotional state and started to explain: "Last week we had a series of special meetings here at the church. The plan was solid. Everything we did was designed for our people to bring their non-Christian friends with them. My worst fears were confirmed. As far as I could tell, out of the two hundred or so who attended, only two of our people brought anyone with them. My conclusion is that their neighbors aren't really their friends."

Many contemporary Christians have abdicated from the world. Often out of good intentions to be "godly," we have confused the biblical injunction to "be separate" with social segregation. We let the activities of our church and relationships with our fellow Christians dominate our lives. We worship together, meet in small groups for Bible study and nurture during the week, and talk on the phone to arrange social events for the weekend. We send our children to Christian schools and depend on each other's older children as our baby sitters. We sense that the world is dangerous to our faith and so we set up subcultures within the larger society. Instead of cultivating significant relationships with people who are outside God's family, we stifle meaningful contact with the very people who would benefit from experiencing life with serious Christians.

This approach to the Christian life counters what Jesus taught during his last week on earth. Jesus knew that his time on this planet was nearing an end, and he left clear instructions for how his followers should relate to the world. Essentially, he said, "Do as I have done." As Jesus prays to his heavenly father on behalf of his disciples, he spells out his directives and expectations. John 17 details the account:

> I will remain in the world no longer, but they are still in the world. . . . They are not of the world any more than I am of the world. My prayer is not that you take them out of the world but that you protect them from the evil one. . . . As you sent me into the world, I have sent them into the world. (vv. 11, 14-15, 18)

If there is confusion about Jesus' teaching, it centers around the meaning of being "not of the world" while being "in the world." Clarity comes when "not of" the world is understood to mean "different from" the world.

In positive terms, the injunction directs God's committed people to get involved in significant ways with people in the world who are not Christians, but also to be known for being qualitatively distinctive. Specifically, developing a reputation among our colleagues and friends for being a generous person will be good news for God, ourselves and our world.

The tragedy of the modern church is that Jesus' strategy for penetrating the culture with the good news of the gospel has been reversed. Instead of being in the world but not of the world, too many of God's committed people are of the world but not in the world. They have been both captured and intimidated by the culture. They have been seduced by the world and have adopted the world's ways as their own—they are "of" the world. They have succumbed to social segregation—they are not "in" the world.

A Better Way

What Jesus demonstrated with Zacchaeus is a better way. His approach still stands as a prototype for faithful and fruitful witnessing in today's society. He took time to be with Zacchaeus. He went into Zacchaeus's comfort zone. Instead of saying, "Come with me, there is a special event at my church" (which is really an invitation to go where Christians are most comfortable), Jesus reversed the norm and surrendered himself to the circumstances where Zacchaeus was most at ease. And while he was with Zacchaeus, Jesus was neither intimidated nor captured. Instead, he engaged Zacchaeus in discussions and decision-making that transformed his whole view of life.

If the church is to be protected from fading further into the backdrop of modern culture, today is the time for those of us who are serious followers of Jesus to get involved with our neighbors, those people who intersect our lives in the natural flow of our days and nights.

The stakes are high. The failure of God's people to live in the world and influence the quality of life in society toward Christian norms will be costly. Almost all of the principal founders of the United States were convinced that the health of the country depended on the moral values derived from religion. In his farewell address, George Washington contended, "Of all the dispositions and habits which lead to political prosperity, religion and morality are indispensable supports."[9] Reflecting on the present and future role of the church in North America, James Reichley proposes, "From the standpoint of the public good, the most important service churches offer to secular life in a free society is to nurture moral values that help humanize capitalism and give direction to democracy."[10]

The subsequent question that confronts North American society is: Can life in a democracy flourish without the stabilizing presence derived from Christian values?

Sometimes Christians are prone to judge the lack of righteousness in the nation. John Stott rightly places the responsibility for the spiritual welfare of every society where it belongs when he asserts: "When any community deteriorates, the blame should be attached where it belongs: not to the community which is going bad but to the church which is failing in its responsibility as salt to stop it going bad."[11]

In response to what Jesus modeled with his life and did on the cross; for the sake of the public good in a secularized free society; out of love for our Lord and commitment to truth—may those of us who call ourselves committed Christians live out the claims of our faith where God has placed us in his world.

Chapter Two

BECOMING MEANING-MAKERS

T*HE WORLD NEEDS TO SEE WHAT THE CHRISTIAN LIFE* looks like. People who think God is unnecessary, or just optional in life, need fresh images of how life is meant to be lived. They need hard evidence that following Jesus really makes a difference. Otherwise, those who have no regard for God will continue to bypass the Christian faith as a worthwhile option.

Lesslie Newbigin, a renowned missiologist, paints Western culture as a pagan society and contends that "its paganism, having been born out of the rejection of Christianity, is far more resistant to the gospel than the pre-Christian paganism with which cross-cultural missions have been familiar."[1]

In order to engage today's world with a credible Christianity, contemporary followers of Jesus will need to be strategic. Injecting fresh meaning into the old gospel will not be achieved by buying more prime-time television or by handing out colored tracts. Rather, the gospel will be perceived as a feasible alternative when those who do not know God have some positive, personal experiences with people who do know him.

Modern Christians have both the privilege of and the potential for becoming spiritual meaning-makers. Of all the people on the face of the earth, followers of Jesus are in the position to make the most sense out of life. Christians have inside information. They have access to the Creator's master plan. Like hooking up a TV channel that has been scrambled, Christians have the capacity to bring a clear picture of what God intended when he set his world in motion. In a society that is barraged with multimessages about what to think and how to live, Christians are the people who can sort out the jumble and chart life with coherent design.

Pray, Care, Communicate

Even with the advantages of being a Christian, maneuvering through the maze of contemporary culture while maintaining a commitment to Christ remains a difficult assignment. Oliver Wendell Holmes is credited with the insight that we need "to get beyond complexity to simplicity." Accordingly, modern Christians need a model of the Christian life that will help us to be both biblically sound and culturally aware.

The following model for modern discipleship keeps a firm hold on the Scriptures while responding to cultural realities. The recommended starting point for living the Christian life in this secular age is simply to *pray, care* and *communicate*.

Pray and experience God.

Care for people and yourself.

Communicate all of God's truth.

The invitation is to be like Jesus. In specific terms, the appeal is to live as Jesus lived and practice what he taught.

Pray

When Jesus was earthbound he developed a reputation for being a man of prayer. On some occasions when his disciples did not know where Jesus had gone, they discovered he had slipped away for some personal time with his heavenly Father. It appears that Jesus' practice of prayer was more frequent than his teaching about the subject. After observing Jesus in prayer one day, his disciples approached him and literally asked, "Lord, teach us to pray" (Lk 11:1).

Jesus' answer to his disciples is still adequate for us today (vv. 2-4). First of all, Jesus said, "When you pray . . ." In offering a pattern for prayer, Jesus provides a structural grid for the content of our prayers.

Be God-focused: pray, "Father." Prayer is an orientation statement for God's people. To pray is to say, "I believe. I believe God exists. I believe I can communicate with him. I believe that he wants to hear from me." The practice of prayer puts us in our place. The heavenly Father is acknowledged as the Creator. Those who pray are the created ones. In a profound sense, God is above. He is the one who deserves the attention and praise.

Be reflective: pray, "Hallowed be your name." Respond to God with an attitude "that he may receive the reverence which his unique character and nature deserve and demand."[2] Reflect on who God is—his trustworthiness, his purity, his brilliance, his convictions, his compassion, his good desires for his world. One of the difficulties with human reflection is that it is often very noisy. The racket of self-interest can destroy the most noble intentions to be contemplative. But at least for a while, the intrusions can be set aside. The mind can be persuaded to think about how God made himself vulnerable by sending Jesus to live with us. Prayer is to know and experience the presence of the living spirit of Christ.

Have a mission concern: pray, "Your kingdom come." Prayer is a statement of intention to take Christ's mission into the world. Prayer is preparation for action; so we will *confess* our inadequacies for the mission, *commit* ourselves to the Lord's calling and *expect* God to be with us as we go forth.

Make petitions: pray, "Give us each day our daily bread." Petitions in prayer are not the recitation of shopping lists. Rather, asking a good God for his favor is a declaration of dependence. Prayer can be jaded by a consumer mentality. Praying can lapse into a blatantly selfish exercise. A healthier posture is to extend the range of prayer to the needs of others. Jesus said we were to pray beyond ourselves. Give "us" our daily bread, not just give "me" my daily bread, was Jesus' counsel. The privilege of prayer is to cradle people and their circumstances in our arms and lift them before the God of the universe.

Confess: pray, "Forgive us our sins." Here is the test of faith in prayer. Here is the great hope of prayer. Dare I believe that my sins can be forgiven? Jesus offers penitent prayer as a form of divine currency. It is a medium that permits transactions between God and his people. In God's economy, confession of sin brings forgiveness. In his mercy, when sin is acknowledged, God grants a reprieve.

Genuine confession is humiliating. Sometimes denying the act of sinning is more attractive than admitting to falling—yet again. C. S. Lewis offers wise counsel:

> No amount of falls will really undo us if we keep on picking ourselves up each time. We shall of course be very muddy and tattered children by the time we reach home. But the bathrooms are all ready, the towels put out, and the clean clothes in the airing cupboard. The only fatal thing is to lose one's temper and give it up. It is when we notice the dirt that God is most present in us: it is the very sign of his presence.[3]

Declare your good intentions: pray, "For we also forgive everyone who sins against us." Don't plan to fall into patterns of sin, like refusing to forgive, but plan to live in a manner that receives God's approval. Jesus knows that the alternative to forgiveness is either overt retaliation or a seething spirit that creates inner sickness. Jesus is saying to his disciples, "Treat the people in your life like God has treated you. Let God's attitude be your attitude. You have been forgiven. Now, extend forgiveness to others."

Plea for protection: pray, "Lead us not into temptation." Jesus knows that living in the world is a dangerous affair. By isolating temptation as a force to be prayed about, Jesus discourages the inclination to become overconfident and self-reliant.

After Jesus teaches his disciples his prayer, he goes on to tell them a parable of prayer.

Suppose one of you has a friend, and he goes to him at midnight and says, "Friend, lend me three loaves of bread, because a friend of mine on a journey has come to me, and I have nothing to set before him."

Then the one inside answers, "Don't bother me. The door is already locked, and my children are with me in bed. I can't get up and give you anything." I tell you, though he will not get up and give him the bread because he is his friend, yet because of the man's boldness he will get up and give him as much as he needs.

So I say to you: Ask and it will be given to you; seek and you will find; knock and the door will be opened to you. For everyone who asks receives; he who seeks finds; and to him who knocks, the door will be opened.

Which of you fathers, if your son asks for a fish, will give him a snake instead? Or if he asks for an egg, will give him a scorpion? If you then, though you are evil, know how to give good gifts to your children, how much more will your Father in heaven give the Holy Spirit to those who ask him! (Lk 11:5-13)

The parable is complex. It contains many messages. There was undoubtedly a question-and-answer session when Jesus finished his statement. The disciples would have wondered, what is most important?

We can summarize the main point by paraphrasing the message this way: "If you want to learn to pray, get to know my Father. Understand who he is and what he is like, and then you will know how to pray. Don't you see how his love exceeds the love of earthly fathers? What he really wants is to give you his Spirit, his own presence. His great gift is himself. He wants a relationship. He wants you to know him and he wants to know you." Prayer from God's point of view is meant to be a "get to know me" encounter.

In the parable, Jesus clearly underscores the importance of persistence in the practice of prayer. Accordingly, he counsels, "Ask, seek, knock—and then the door will be opened to you."

What does it mean to be persistent? In the Christian circles I move around in, there is an emphasis on having a daily quiet time. The emphasis is right. Days that begin with a focused time with God and input from the Scriptures are like well-tuned musical instruments, ready to be performed upon. Everyone in the concert hall of life is better off.

But even though I know the value of a consistent quiet time and affirm the practice, the truth is, my record is suspect. Over the years I have bought more devotional books and helps than I care to confess. My experiments at spurring consistency have been many, and at times, even creative. My long-term struggle to maintain a strong devotional life has led to this conclusion: It is important to find your spiritual rhythm.

An image from the Psalms which encourages a daily quiet time is:
As the deer pants for streams of water
  so my soul pants for you, O God.
My soul thirsts for God, for the living God.
  When can I go and meet with God? (Ps 42:1-2)
For many expositors the answer to that question is "early in the morning." We should be like deer, rising early to go and drink. After all, Jesus got up at dawn to go and pray, didn't he? The logic sounds so right. But what if you are a night person rather than a morning person?

What if God made you more like a night-riding camel than a deer?

God does not manufacture human clones. Neither does he have the same prayer expectations for everyone who pledges loyalty to him. God does not treat everyone the same way. That approach would depersonalize the relationship. At the same time, God does desire communion with members of his family. And on the human side, we need systematic and repeated time with the Father. Otherwise, our commitment to the relationship becomes suspect.

When it comes to personal prayer, daily or otherwise, you need to find your rhythm. Based on who you are and the realities of your scheduled commitments, determine what works for you. And then persevere in the practice of prayer. Be like the friend at the door in the night. Keep knocking until there is an answer.

The Holy Spirit also brings an eternal perspective into the present tense of daily affairs. Days and nights are attached to heaven and hell. The Spirit prompts those in Christ to interpret the present in the context of what God has done in the past and what he promises to do in the future.

This awareness of God in us brings a supernatural orientation into our frame of reference. We taste his personal presence. We experience being "a new creation in Christ." We are a miracle. We believe in miracles. We expect God to overrule the natural with his supernatural intervention.

Prayer is part of our being partners with God in the whole process of making him known. Prayer for specific people prompts God to speak to them. The Holy Spirit arouses spiritual interest and convicts people of their sin. Praying for people lifts the level of our concern for them. Our elevated awareness of people's needs prompts us to care for them. When prayer is part of the flow of life toward people around us, God gives us insight to communicate his truth with sensitivity and spiritual power. We become energized and motivated to reach out. We are prompted to engage in discussions with the people in our lives who need to pursue God and his ways.

Care

Although prayer is indispensable to healthy Christian living, it is only one part of experiencing life in Christ. In the proposed model for modern discipleship—pray, care, communicate—praying is like one leg of a three-legged stool. Without prayer, the Christian life is off balance and unstable. But neither can the Christian life be simply reduced to the practice of prayer. By itself, prayer becomes a form of self-indulgence that does not engage the world.

By contrast, tangible acts of caring and kindness do get the attention of the world. Especially in these times, when self-interest controls so much of society's agenda, caring for the people God brings into our lives brings the light of heaven into the darkness of our present world.

I learned about care from a friend early one Sunday morning. I was in an airport a long way from home. As I sauntered toward the departure gate, someone called out my name. Recovering from the unexpected interruption, I turned and recognized a face, but not a name. The man reintroduced himself as Greg. We had met at a conference a few years earlier. We exchanged greetings, wandered through a little surface conversation and then I inquired, "Greg, what are you doing here at this time of the morning?"

Greg sighed a little. "It's sort of a long story. I have an old friend Robert who is not doing very well. We grew up together and then parted ways. I hadn't heard from him for ten years or so. A few months ago, he and his family walked back into my life. Frankly, Robert is an alcoholic who is on the verge of losing it all—his wife and kids, his house, his profession and whatever else he has on this earth. I came down early this morning to wire him a plane ticket. He doesn't get in for another five hours."

"What happens when Robert arrives?" I asked.

"Well," Greg answered, "the plan is to let him move in with my wife Cindy and me for three or four months. We think he just needs to be protected and supported for a while. He's agreed to go to AA. We hope he'll come to church with us. Maybe he can get it back together. We really don't know if it will work, but we're going to try."

We said our good-bys and I boarded my plane. I was captured by what Greg and Cindy were doing. What a powerful statement for the gospel. But what an inordinate cost. I prayed that Robert would be restored and that God would honor their good efforts. I sat back in my seat and thought about Jesus' teaching to "love your neighbor as yourself" and mused that the good Samaritan was still alive. Thank God!

The costly care that Greg and his wife expressed toward Robert and his family is hard evidence of the energizing Holy Spirit in their lives. God not only shaped Greg and Cindy's values so they were open to respond to Robert, but he helped them feel secure enough to get involved. Too frequently, serious followers of Jesus are not able to care for people around them who have needs because they are insecure in themselves.

Engaging the culture with a credible gospel in this age will need to convey meaning about where "self" fits into the whole scheme of things. The world is excessively preoccupied with self, and Christians are frequently confused about the subject.

If any group has the right of access to a positive self-image, it is Christian believers who are created "in the image of God" and have subsequently been redeemed and re-created to live "in Christ."

However, the invitation to the abundant life promised in Christ is often derailed by false teaching and overzealous desires to be "spiritual." On numerous occasions I have asked people, "Why have you stopped coming to church?" The responses have been revealing. Frequently people have said, "When the church keeps telling me 'You are evil. You are sinful,' I end up feeling ugly and worthless. Don't ask me to go back to that." Somehow, these people have got the message that to be *sinful* is to be *worthless*. As well as demeaning their self-images, their misunderstanding has turned them away from the church and from God. They need to grasp the message that Jesus only died because *those who have sinned do have ultimate worth in Christ.*

A paraphrase of the definition of love in 1 Corinthians 13:4-5 provides further guidance for developing a healthy self-concept: "Love and care for yourself. Be patient and kind to yourself. Watch out for envy and pride. Accept who you are without the need to boast. Live so you deserve self-respect. Avoid the abuse of being rude toward yourself. Give yourself permission to fail without excessive remorse. Accept God's forgiveness and forgive yourself when you do wrong."

In Jesus' teaching, self-love is never isolated from both love for God and love for your neighbor (Lk 10:25-28). For the Christian, the expression of love flows within a triangle of relationships. God is the source of all love. Part of the image of God in his creation is the inherent capacity to love. A consequence of living "in Christ" is the enhanced ability to love. A healthy and balanced Christian life only results when love and care are expressed in all three directions—to God, to yourself and to the people in your life.

In telling the parable of the good Samaritan, Jesus discloses what's involved in neighbor-loving or caring for the people in your life (Lk 10:29-37). The story is familiar. A man is stripped and beaten by thieves. As the man is lying abandoned and wounded on the side of the road, first a priest and then a Levite pass him by. Finally, a Samaritan stops, bandages the man's wounds, takes him to an inn, cares for him and leaves payment for the man's stay while he recovers.

Caring presumes value. The Samaritan is always given full marks for being compassionate. Unlike the others who had already passed by, "he took pity" on the man who had been robbed and injured (v. 33). Why did he stop? What were his values? He had a higher priority for people, and particularly people in need, than he had for the immediate demands of his personal schedule. He could not pass by and still be comfortable with himself. The choice "to care or not to care, to love or not to love" is not necessarily contingent on the presence of a perceived need. The first two passersby also perceived a need. But compassion flows from within, out of a deeper reality. The urge to encourage someone in despair is prompted by internal values. We need to decide right here, right now, that we will be care-givers and lovers.

Caring costs. In modern parlance, the Samaritan used his St. John's first-aid training to handle the initial medical emergency. Then he pulled out his American Express card to cover the costs of a couple of nights in the local Holiday Inn (vv. 34-35). Whether an act of care is writing a careful letter of reference or letting someone live with you until he or she finds an apartment, it costs. And often the cost involves what is most valuable to us—time and money. Jesus portrays the Samaritan giving both.

Caring addresses disparity. In the parable, the Samaritan is the strong person with the resources while the victim in the ditch is weak and needy. In this world, equality is a myth. If you use yourself as a comparative reference point, some people around you will always be more gifted, more intelligent and more compassionate. On the other side of the comparison, other people will have less capacity than you in those same categories. People who are born with high energy levels are not better people, but they do have a decided advantage in a competitive society. People who are born with disabilities and others who suffer serious injuries in accidents have to overcome handicaps before they get to the starting line of success in life. Acts of love and care begin to address the disparities in this world.

Several years ago I watched a young woman push a young man in a wheelchair into a crowded lobby. His body was paralyzed and almost motionless. She was a picture of vibrant life. They shared lunch together in that open forum. The woman positioned her friend so she could look directly into his eyes. She fed him a sandwich, one bite at a time. As they ate, they talked and enjoyed each other. When the meal was finished, the young woman reached into her purse and lit a cigarette. She proceeded to repeatedly place the cigarette between his lips and take it back again until it was almost gone. For those moments, the rest of the world was blocked out. Their whole encounter had a sense of dignity about it.

Caring brings life. Whether people are Christians or not, their caring brings life. Jesus said it best. After the lawyer recited the commandment to "love . . . God . . . and love your neighbor as yourself," Jesus challenged him: "Do this and you will live" (vv. 27-28). The obvious antitheses is, "If you do not love, you will die."

Caring authenticates belief claims. People who have rejected Jesus and his teachings feel that they have no obligation to obey his commandments. Genuine Christians do not have the same prerogative. They are obligated to translate Jesus' teachings into tangible behavior. For followers of Jesus, aiming to love and care for people is as basic to the Christian life as breathing and eating is to physical well-being. To think and do otherwise is to betray the essence of faith.

Caring incites belief. Following the end of the Vietnam War, thousands of Christians in the Western world opened their homes and their lives to the needs of Vietnamese refugees. In contrast to the horror of the war, the response of God's people and others who offered their resources stood as a symbol of hope.

Recently, one Christian campus worker reported that a Vietnamese student had seen an advertisement for a Bible study and had just joined the group on campus. The reason the student started to study the Bible is what is significant. His words are profound: "I must find out more about your God, because you are the people who helped my people."

When the people who call themselves Christians express care and love in this world, their behavior rings with Christlikeness. Caring not only authenticates the claim to be Christian, it awakens people to how beautiful life can be and prompts them to consider the Savior.

Communicate

Even the combination of praying and caring for people's needs make up only two legs on a three-legged stool. Praying and demonstrating God's truth by caring for people need to be complemented with the articulation of his truth. Careful words of witness give meaning to

Christ's death and resurrection. Verbal silence keeps God's good news a secret.

The grave difficulty of communicating God's truth in these times is that modern society doesn't believe in truth anymore. Previous assumptions that objective truth exists and can be known have been set aside. Former categories for truth have been dismantled and scrapped.

In 1987, Allan Bloom began his influential book *The Closing of the American Mind* with the following statement: "There is one thing a professor can be absolutely certain of: almost every student entering the university believes, or says he believes, that truth is relative."[4] Bloom sees today's students as being indoctrinated to believe that relativism is a "condition of a free society" and consequently, there is "virtue in openness. . . . There are no absolutes; freedom is absolute."[5]

In this milieu, one person's point of view is just as valid as another person's perspective. Making an appeal to an external reference point like God is all right if that is how you want to view the world, but that is just one of many views. It is a right of your freedom to think that way, but it has no real merit beyond being one idea among other ideas.

How do we communicate that God's good news is more than a lifestyle option? How do we communicate that God's revelation of his Son is ultimate truth, a truth that goes beyond mere subjective experience, intuition or personal preference?

When Jesus was articulating his teachings on earth, he was neither sharing his feelings nor simply expressing his personal opinions. Rather, he was making known what his Father in heaven had already revealed to him. In situations when he was asked questions, his answers were not manufactured out of the deep insight of his superior I.Q. Rather, his responses were restatements of God's truth as it applied to particular subjects and circumstances. We can regard Jesus' modus operandi demonstrated in Luke 10:25-42 as a model for us.

Communicate in context. When a lawyer in the audience posed the question, "What must I do to inherit eternal life?" Jesus did not launch into a three-point sermon. He knew he was being scrutinized and tested. He answered the inquiry with a two-part question: "What is written in the law?" and "How do you read it?" The dialog continued like a fencing match between Jesus and the lawyer until Jesus told the parable of the Samaritan (vv. 25-37).

Jesus' response in his encounter with the lawyer is a prototype for how he communicated God's truth. Jesus repeatedly used the circumstances in a situation to convey what he wanted to communicate. The pattern was the same in Mary and Martha's home. When Martha interrupted the conversation that Jesus and Mary were having in the living room to chastise Mary for not helping in the kitchen, Jesus challenged Martha's priorities (Lk 10:38-42).

Tell the truth creatively. Jesus' ability to contextualize his truth kept him from being boring. Dorothy Sayers offers a timely reminder: "The people who hanged Christ never . . . accused him of being a bore. . . . Jesus was emphatically not a dull man in his human lifetime, and if he was God, there can be nothing dull about God either."[6] Jesus' engaging style becomes evident as we analyze the passages in Luke 10 and 11 that we covered above.

1. Jesus asked questions. After telling the parable of the Samaritan, Jesus invited a response from the lawyer with the question, "Who do you think was a neighbor?" In the parable about prayer, questions were part of the fabric of the story. "Which of you fathers, if your son asks for a fish, will give him a snake instead?" Jesus repeatedly solicited responses from his audience so he could interact with them.

2. He told stories. Jesus excelled at the art of storytelling. He knew that visual memories in the minds of his listeners could be recalled and retold. He understood the power of the parable to invite identification and create intrigue. He recognized that anecdotes and analogies could capture minds. And so Jesus looked at

life and crafted stories and developed metaphors. He communicated in color. He had the God-given ability to speak with clarity but still leave enough room for reading between the lines.

3. He provoked responses. A study of Jesus' methods of communication leads to the conclusion that he was out to convert passive listeners. He knew when to turn the conversation and when to stop talking. Jesus did not give prepackaged speeches when he talked. He sensed the right moment to draw the line and then waited for a response.

In the case of the lawyer, Jesus interacted and, I think, enjoyed the verbal duel. Then, after the lawyer flawlessly quoted the Old Testament commandment to love, Jesus pressed his point. "You have answered correctly," was Jesus' reply; but he didn't stop there. He gave the lawyer something to think about long into the night: "Do this and you will live" (10:27-28).

In the comfort of Mary and Martha's home, Jesus was not as confrontational, but neither was he apologetic. Martha set the tone for the encounter when she pushed the blame for being alone in the kitchen toward Jesus.

"Lord, don't you care that my sister has left me to do the work by myself? Tell her to help me!"

"Martha, Martha," the Lord answered, "you are worried and upset about many things, but only one thing is needed. Mary has chosen what is better." (10:38-42)

With tenderness, he provoked Martha into rethinking her priorities.

Jesus was not driven to making impressive, lofty-sounding speeches. Rather, he engaged his audience. He aroused interest and provoked responses. He had the capacity to identify with the people and the issues that dominated the situation.

Use relational influence. People in significant relationships are not only free to communicate convincingly with each other, they influence each other. Truth-telling in this age is most persuasive when people who are talking to each other really know each other. Jesus' interaction with Martha and Mary took place in their home, and their friendship was strong enough for Martha to be forthright.

Jesus' style of relating and communicating God's truth is a pattern for us too. Just as Jesus adapted his way of truth-telling to fit the people and circumstances in his situations, we can learn to do the same. Asking appropriate questions still opens doors into people's lives. Jesus told stories, and we have stories to tell too. The whole Bible is a story of how God has loved and sought the love of his human creation. The life and death and resurrection of Jesus deserves to be retold over and over. And we have our own stories to tell about how God has reshaped who we are. Jesus' use of his imagination to create his many parables is an open invitation for us to conceive new ways to tell old truth. Provoking responses instead of simply conveying information is more difficult, but God's Spirit will be our helper, especially if we are attempting to communicate as Jesus did.

Depending on the Holy Spirit

Combining the practices of praying and experiencing God, caring for people, and communicating the full scope of God's truth shows the world what the Christian life is like. It also brings a sense of coherence to the Christian life. As a strategy for living in today's world, it unscrambles the distorted images of what the Christian looks like.

The complexities of modern life and the inadequacies of even the best of our human endeavors will press us who want to reach out to our friends and neighbors to *depend on the Holy Spirit.* The presence of the Holy Spirit in God's people is not just a noble idea. The Holy Spirit is energy for living the Christian life. Without God's energy in his people, Christianity is nothing more than a sophisticated human enterprise. It is the activity of the Holy Spirit in transformed people that translates the theory of the Christian faith into the practice of Christian living.

A friend of mine had a chance to practice his faith when he was confounded by a personal problem and a friend's dilemma. He was praying as he drove down the highway with two problems agitating his mind. The transmission in his car was close to mechanical failure. And one of his colleagues was facing unusual financial pressure. He had already secured two estimates on the cost to repair the transmission and really had no option but to make an appointment and pay the four hundred dollars. As my friend cruised along the road at sixty-five miles per hour, the Holy Spirit interjected a thought.

"Why not ask God to play mechanic? After all, if he can create the world, surely he can fix a transmission. Then you can give the money to your colleague."

Being both impulsive and imaginative, my friend reacted with immediate excitement. "That's it," he thought. "What a deal. People are more important than things. God can act and the money can go for something really worthwhile." He began to pray and ask God to act.

Without taking his foot off the accelerator, my friend and God had a party. It was a rare moment. The Spirit spoke. My friend listened. He was confident enough that God had literally healed his transmission that he wrote a check made out to his colleague. (He secretly confessed that he held the check for two weeks—just to be sure.)

Several months and 15,000 miles later I checked with my friend about the condition of the transmission. He grinned. "Working like a charm, and I haven't had to take it back for any warranty work."

Experiencing God verifies the theory of faith. It injects an undeniable certainty that is persuasive and compelling. When your confidence in God is high, you are bound to be more enthusiastic for the faith. When God has just made himself known to you, even if the majority of society is disregarding him, your reality of faith stands tall. No one can take your experience with God away from you.

A natural extension of experiencing God is to expect others around you to experience him too. God is not the personal property of a chosen few. To know him is to realize he wants to extend himself where he is neither known nor welcomed.

Still, there is no complete formula for living the Christian life or for witnessing in a manner that guarantees results. Praying for people could very well activate God's Spirit in their lives and raise our awareness of their spiritual and physical needs, but it will not ensure their entering the kingdom. Caring in practical ways for individuals around us will be a statement of Christ's love in us, but it will not necessarily lead to their finding new life in Christ.

When God's people pray, care and communicate, they send the right signals to the watching world. They are perceived by the world to have credibility. When non-Christians see consistency and coherence in Christians around them, they are attracted. Those who observe meaning in others become thirsty for meaning themselves. Even when people choose to reject the faith for themselves, the integrity of the Christian lifestyle still solicits respect.

So as we seek to reach others for Christ, we need to acknowledge who God is and accept who we are. We must bow our heads and hearts in humility and pray to be used for some good purpose on this earth. As we pray, care and communicate, we must let God be God. It is up to us only to cooperate with his endeavors. Christ is the one who redeems.

Chapter Three

OVERCOMING INTIMIDATION

I *SENSED AN INNER URGE TO REACH UP AND TAKE OFF* my name tag. I wanted to go incognito and blend into the crowd. I didn't want anyone to know I was a Christian. I felt emotionally intimidated.

The setting for my trauma was the Calgary Stampede grounds (the site of the 1988 winter Olympics). I was one of the speakers at a Christian festival. The planners had hoped 30,000 of God's people would witness to the world and experience an inspiring celebration. In the end, less than half that number showed up.

Despite all the advance planning no one had thought of the unlikely possibility that the Calgary Flames would be playing the Stanley

Cup finals on the same site at the same time.

The festival got off to a slow start. The evening rallies were held in the old corral where hockey games used to be played. The capacity of the building was approximately 7,000 people. The first night close to 2,500 people showed their name tags to the ushers and seated themselves on the lower level. The empty bleachers towered over the audience like a high-rise looking down on a house. No one said anything, but everyone secretly wished the crowd had been larger— much larger. The leaders on the platform did their best to convey enthusiasm. The speakers charged their words with conviction. But disappointment prevailed. It's hard to celebrate when the chairs are half empty.

The National Hockey League finals for the Stanley Cup were played in the Saddledome, a new facility located less than a hundred yards from the old corral. When all the seats are filled, more than 17,000 people can cheer for their favorite teams.

One evening that weekend both events were going on simultaneously. I was making my way toward the entrance of the old corral. I knew it would be more empty than full. The main flow of the crowd was headed for the Saddledome and the big game. Even the standing-room spaces had been sold. To be truthful, I wished I had been able to get a ticket. I even contemplated trying to make a deal with one of the scalpers. As I was being pushed along by the crowd I had a strong sense that God was not winning in this world. In my heart I knew I didn't want to be known as one of those religious types. That was the moment when I wanted to take off my name tag.

I'm certainly not offering my experience as a statement of virtue. It is simply an illustration of what can happen in this age. As serious followers of Jesus, committed and convinced that the Bible is true and Christianity is valid, we can still be pushed around by what is going on in today's society. We can be psychologically intimidated. And when intimidation strikes, most of us are more inclined to run away or hide in silence than we are to speak out and stand tall for our Lord.

The Grasshopper Syndrome

The Bible reveals that intimidation is not a new force in the world. There have been others who have wanted to take off their name tags too. The apostle Peter made great claims of allegiance to Jesus but he folded under pressure. His desire to support Jesus was noble, but the circumstances of that fateful night around the campfire pushed him into denying he was even associated with his Lord (Lk 22:54-62). There is a graphic account of the same phenomenon in Numbers 13. The people involved are the twelve Hebrew spies who were sent on a reconnaissance mission and instructed to bring back a report on life in the land of Canaan.

The plan was God's idea. "The LORD said to Moses, 'Send some men to explore the land of Canaan, which I am giving to the Israelites' " (v. 1). God was very specific with Moses. "Send one leader from each of the twelve tribes." Moses did exactly as God directed and developed his list of twelve worthy representatives (vv. 4-16).

Moses was also very specific when he called the twelve together for their briefing session:

Go up through the Negev and on into the hill country. See what the land is like and whether the people who live there are strong or weak, few or many. What kind of land do they live in? Is it good or bad? What kind of towns do they live in? Are they unwalled or fortified? How is the soil? Is it fertile or poor? Are there trees on it or not? Do your best to bring back some of the fruit of the land. (vv. 17-20)

The twelve leaders did as they were told. They followed the map as they explored the land. They took notes. They made their estimates. They cut down large clusters of fresh grapes and for good measure they brought along some pomegranates too. The mission took them a total of forty days, and then they returned to the desert where Moses and the Israelites were waiting for their report (vv. 21-26).

After Moses and Aaron and others welcomed their men back, they sampled the fruit and the debriefing began.

> We went into the land to which you sent us, and it does flow with milk and honey! Here is its fruit. But the people who live there are powerful, and the cities are fortified and very large. . . . We can't attack those people; *they are stronger than we are.* (vv. 27-28, 31; emphasis mine)

Initially, the majority report had only one dissenter and he was not about to remain silent. Caleb forcefully broke into the proceedings: "We should go up and take possession of the land, for *we certainly can do it"* (v. 30; emphasis mine).

Caleb's minority perspective did not carry much weight with the others. Although he was able to convince Joshua to join his cause, the Israelites voted to go with the majority. The prospect of staying in the desert or facing defeat led to grumbling and despair. The whole assembly turned on Moses and rebelled against God. The growing consensus was to go back to Egypt rather than ahead to Canaan (Num 14:1-4). The consequences proved to be severe. God's plan was put on hold and the whole nation stayed marooned in the desert for another forty years.

The key to understanding the point of view of the majority report is profoundly stated in Numbers 13:33. Thinking about the people they were strategizing to conquer, the spies said of themselves, *"We seemed like grasshoppers in our own eyes, and we looked the same to them"* (emphasis mine).

They had been intimidated by the giants in the land. They were captured by their circumstances without remembering that God was with them. Their past triumphs—the plagues in Egypt, the parting of the sea, the manna to eat—stayed filed in their memory banks. Their confidence crumbled. Their self-images went limp. The best they could do was identity with grasshoppers: "We are small; they are big. We are weak; they are strong. We will lose; they will win. Let's go back; we can't do it."

The majority of the spies were simply overwhelmed. With the human odds stacked against them, they began to read life with grasshopper eyes. They not only imagined themselves as small and inadequate, they thought the giants saw them as weaklings too. The opposition was too strong. The only alternative was to retreat and back away.

There are forces operating in the world today that are triggering shades of the grasshopper syndrome in many of God's people. Many Christians feel weak and reticent about being visible in our culture. They really want to love and serve God, but they feel intimidated.

Silenced by Social Pressure

All Christians feel this pressure to be silent. Christian high-schoolers may be faithful church attenders, worshiping in the pew on Sunday morning, studying the Bible, praying, going on retreat weekends. But during the week at their local high school, these same young people are silent about their church involvement and professed faith in Christ. Their parents sometimes encourage their teen-agers to get involved in the Christian group that operates in their school. Instead of admitting to peer pressure and how religious types are viewed by the majority of their fellow students, these Christian young people make statements to their parents like, "Do you know what kind of people go to that group? They're a bunch of losers. There is no way I'm becoming a part of that group. I'd rather be dead!" The conversation usually ends at that point. Some mothers and fathers realize the explanation is really an excuse to take cover from the prevailing social pressures.

University students who have noble intentions to be loyal to Jesus and to stand for him are shrinking back into quietness about their personal faith too. For example, a program may call for an open forum to publicly proclaim the gospel. A gifted guest speaker is invited and profiled. The aim is to gather a crowd and stimulate questions between the audience and the speaker. Part of the strategy is to have Christians from the sponsoring group present before the speaking begins. They know that after a small group is gathered, others passing by feel safe about joining in. Members of the group are encouraged to be there themselves and to bring their friends. The time arrives for the microphones to be turned on and the speaker to be introduced. But only a small percentage of the members of the group are present, and even the majority of the planners are absent. What's gone wrong?

The giants are strong. The forces of intimidation are real. In the campus environment, the external social pressure not to identify with Christ in public is more powerful than the internal commitment to represent Christ overtly.

Adults from many sectors of the society are embarrassed in both private and public situations to identify themselves as serious followers of Jesus too. They relate to the world as perfectly harmless Christians.

Once I found myself interpreting today's youth to a large group of public-school educators. In the flow of the session, I followed my practice of deliberately critiquing a segment of the research data in a manner that revealed my personal Christian perspective. At the end of the morning, I was invited to join the planning committee and the superintendent of schools for lunch.

The lunch was a pleasant affair, but what happened after we had finished eating was the most memorable. We left the dining room and were headed to the parking lot when the superintendent took me aside for a private conversation. He expressed his appreciation for the morning presentation, including the integration of the spiritual dimension, and then he said quietly: "I also wanted you to know that I teach an adult Sunday-school class at my church."

We ended our discussion, but my mind kept asking questions. What factors force the person in charge of a whole school division to hide his Christian identity from his colleagues? Why didn't he utilize the conversation time over lunch as an opportunity to return to some of the spiritual content of the morning session? Why do successful and well-adjusted adults have to whisper their religious messages to another Christian so that no one else will hear?

Religion Is Off-Limits

Bill Diehl, a management consultant who has worked in the corporate business world for the past forty years, reflects on what has stopped him from initiating spiritually related conversations with his business associates:

> In one sense, nothing; in a larger sense, everything. It simply was not part of corporate culture to talk religion. In the same way no one had to tell you not to wear tennis shoes to work, or forget to shave, no one had to say that religion is an off-limits subject in this corporation. We all knew it.[1]

Why is religion off-limits? Why is there reticence in so many people to speak about the reality of God in their lives in natural situations? What are the reasons that cause serious followers of Jesus to feel like they are grasshoppers living in a land inhabited by giants?

No one ever called a news conference to formalize the announcement, but there is a prevailing consensus in North American society that God is unnecessary. In subtle whispers and with bold accolades the culture chants, "You do not need God. You do not need God." And when you hear the same message over and over again, at least at an unconscious level, you begin to believe it.

The idea that God is not central in this world is seeded in your mind before your feet hit the floor in the morning. The preset alarm on the bedside radio brings you the news from the night before. There's an update on a war going on somewhere. Closer to home there has been an overnight rape and murder, firefighters are containing a blaze at a paint factory, and there is no end in sight for the strike that is in its fourteenth day. The news concludes with a little political rhetoric, a human interest snapshot, a short weather report, a long sports report and a warning about a serious accident that has caused a major traffic tie-up. God is never mentioned. He doesn't matter.

God has not been declared dead in the modern world, he has just been displaced. God is the forgotten one, on the sidelines of everyday life. Certainly, many would admit, he still exists. It's just that he is . . .

unnecessary. Optional. In our culture's eyes, God has lost his creator-clout.

Watch an evening of TV sitcoms and count the number of permissive sexual innuendos. Study the lyrics of the songs on the charts in the top 40. Scan the movie page in the paper and analyze the messages. Walk into a major book store and count the number of "self-help" and "how to" titles on the shelves. Then go to the religious section and compare the count. Look at best-seller lists and find out what is selling. Monitor the number of times in a week that the media invites you to indulge yourself. Contrast the frequency of those invitations with the times you are encouraged to give yourself away in response to someone else's needs.

Listen to the pulse of society. Note the repeated references to dollars and economics, to profits and losses. Spend a Sunday afternoon in a shopping center and ponder why the Lord's Day is so much like the other days of the week. Think about how the media typecasts members of the clergy in television and movie productions.

Scrutinize the society. Go out into the world and take a deep breath. Inhale the culture. Then ask, "What is central? What priorities dominate? When our world plans and talks and dreams, what is on the agenda? And what place is given to God?"

God has been demoted. Science and technology have been elevated to his place, securing the place of trust and confidence that used to be reserved for religion. Faith in God has been swapped for faith in human ingenuity.

Computers represent a powerful example of the scientific surge into the grassroots of society. Douglas Webster projects some of the consequences:

> Modern men and women look to computers and to the individual "self" for spiritual deliverance. The contemporary sacred hope is in computers, a modern Baal, absorbing our energies and passions in much the same way that the ancient god of fertility compromised Israel's devotion to Yahweh. . . . No wonder it is difficult to speak

of God in Christ to this generation. It is difficult to speak of Christ convincingly even to Christians.[2]

Another measure of our current state as a society is found in professor Neil Postman's book *Amusing Ourselves to Death.* Postman suggests that at different times in history, specific cities have been the focal point for the prevailing spirit in America. In the late eighteenth century, Boston was the center of a political radicalism that ignited a shot heard around the world. In the midnineteenth century, New York became the symbol of the idea of a melting-pot America. Chicago was the city of "big shoulders and heavy winds" that came to represent the industrial energy in the early part of the twentieth century.

Today's metaphor of American character and aspiration is Las Vegas, Nevada, says Postman. "[It] is a city entirely devoted to the idea of entertainment, and as such proclaims the spirit of a culture in which all public discourse increasingly takes the form of entertainment." Postman reasons, "In America God favors all those who possess both a talent and a format to amuse, whether they be preachers, athletes, entrepreneurs, politicians, teachers or journalists."[3]

Postman's discernment dramatically declares how unchristian North American society has become. The problem is not that entertainment is evil or that being amused is immoral. It is a question of what orientation dominates a culture. When entertainment is the primary motif, the feeding of self is high on the agenda of life. When a thirst for amusement describes the spirit of the age, the pursuit of personal pleasure mandates the culture.

Why can't we talk about God? Why do we feel like the world is winning? The social pressures and values of our modern times trigger spiritual intimidation, and many of God's good people become casualties. Instead of planning to engage the culture and take the land, the tendency is to pull back and protect the territory that is already in possession. Retreat is appealing. Silence is safer. Withdrawal seems wiser.

There are giants in our land, and they intimidate us. The drive to be self-sufficient, the secularization of our society, and the minority status Christians hold today all send us into hiding, trembling.

Beyond Self-Sufficiency

One of the tragic realities of our society is that we are taught and re-taught that we can make it on our own. Self-sufficiency is applauded in our culture. Depending on others is a sign of weakness. Being open about needing God to help cope with the pressures of life is in poor taste. Our culture programs us for self-reliance. The propaganda is preached incessantly, and unless we reprogram our self-understand-ings, we will begin believing we are strong enough to make it on our own.

Psychology has traditionally reinforced the message of self-suffi-ciency. One of the proponents of this message is Abraham Maslow, whose hierarchy of basic human needs is common in psychology textbooks. His premise is that lower needs must be satisfied before higher needs can be fulfilled. Maslow's grid begins with the "survival needs" of physical life, moves to the need for "safety and security," followed by the need for "belongingness and affection," which leads to the need for "self-esteem." It culminates with the prospect of "self-actualization."

Maslow's model is helpful in understanding human behavior. If you have not eaten for two days, you are not likely to choose stimu-lating conversation over food. Where Maslow's hierarchy falls short, however, is in its overestimation of human ability. It leads us to believe that *we* possess the resources to "self-actualize."

Maslow is not the only one to esteem humanity so highly. Leo Buscaglia, author, speaker and university professor, has been a lead-ing prophet of the human potential movement. With his fingers rest-ing on the pulse of the populace, "Dr. Hug" articulates what people want to hear about themselves and how they want to be perceived by others. He has given society a creed that fuels its drive to be self-sufficient.

Buscaglia's genius is that he eclectically chooses what is central to the Christian faith—love, respect, valuing others—and then weaves his teaching into the design of creation. He agrees with God at critical points. His teaching has the ring of truth.

But he does not tell the whole truth—and therein lies Buscaglia's deceit. He fails to account for the dark side of human character. His approach does not calculate the impact of sin and the results of being alienated from God. He expects too much from people who don't have access to Christ's resources. Buscaglia doesn't acknowledge that the practice of loving is too often overruled by the stronger presence of selfishness and self-interest. In the end, the human potential movement makes promises that it cannot keep.

The challenge for the Christian is to live in this culture without believing the propaganda preached by it. The "I am strong enough on my own" message will continue to be chanted in our society. Christians who do not resist the teaching will be attracted to it. The idea of being autonomous will be alluring. In the push and pull of life, God will continue to offer himself to his people. Some will go the way of the ten spies; others will follow the example of Caleb and Joshua.

What separated Caleb and Joshua from the others? An assessment of why ten of the twelve leaders were intimidated when they spied out the land of Canaan is revealing. The problem did not lie with the spies' suitability for their assignment. As persons, they had credibility with their peers. They were solid citizens. They were considered as worthy spiritual representatives of their tribes. Moses was a competent leader. He would not have chosen them if he was not confident they could handle the assignment.

So what happened to these good people? Why did they fail? Why was their faith in the future crushed? The answer rests in isolating how Caleb and Joshua were different from the ten. While the intimidated ten were lobbying their tribes to dump Moses and choose a new leader to take them back to Egypt, Caleb and Joshua were pleading with the people to head for the land of Canaan (Num 14:1-9). Joshua and Caleb did not base their appeal on a master military plan. Rather, they were staking their future on the same God who had been with them in the past. They remembered the Red Sea. Listen to their rationale:

> If the LORD is pleased with us, he will lead us into the land, a land flowing with milk and honey, and will give it to us. Only do not rebel against the LORD. And do not be afraid of the people of the land, because we will swallow them up. Their protection is gone, but the LORD is with us. (vv. 8-9)

Caleb and Joshua held on to God's vision for the future because they held on to God. The intimidated ten lost sight of what the future could be because they slipped along the way and became spiritually self-sufficient. God did not fit into their plans. They made their calculations without God in the equation. And regardless of their gifts and ingenuity, they were not strong enough on their own to achieve what God had designed for them.

The dynamics remain the same today. Embracing self-sufficiency is still a major move toward spiritual ineffectiveness. The people God can use are not those who claim to be strong and invincible. The self-sufficient are always left to their self-made vulnerability. They over-believe in their own strength and set themselves up to come tumbling down. The paradox is that without God's resources they end up under-achieving.

Caleb and Joshua, on the other hand, were used by God because they knew their limits and kept their confidence in God's resources. They had eyes to see what God wanted to achieve. Their message to the people was "With God, we can do it." Their confidence in God was stronger than the prevailing social pressures around them. They were ready to go and stand up to the giants in the land.

Secularization

Cousin to self-sufficiency in the roster of cultural trends is the move toward secularization in our society. "The seclusion of many realms of life from religious influence,"[4] as J. Russell Hale calls it, is a process which happens over time. A culture that is historically built on the Judeo-Christian foundation of God's values and ethics cannot be secularized overnight. The conversion has been happening over decades.

Secular people are those whose life simply has no room for God; they are people who "have shoved religion to the sidelines. Religious ideas and religious institutions have absolutely no impact on how [these] people spend their money, use their time, watch television or run their businesses,"[5] writes Glenn Smith, an urban ministry specialist. J. Russell Hale describes secularists as those "who embrace worldliness in the sense that the dignity or worth of people lies in their capacity for self-realization through reason, without benefit of clergy, or of the church."[6]

Even our TV sitcoms help to secularize us. The quintessential secularists are the Huxtable family members on "The Bill Cosby Show." Mom and Dad are college graduates, both making it in the professional world. One is a lawyer and the other a medical doctor; their standard of living spells out their success. Their marriage is strong. Their love for each other is compelling. The subject of sex is given just the right touch. Expensive paintings adorn the walls of their comfortable home. The presence of five children provide the setting to parade all the normal problems of growing up inside a stable family. Creativity and cleverness mark the problem-solving. Humor and laughter flavor the whole affair.

But God is absent. Nothing derogatory about God is ever implied. He is simply not necessary and doesn't make it into the script. As an example, when Thanksgiving was the theme for a particular episode, instead of a prayer before the meal, each member of the family was asked to share something that made them thankful. God didn't make it onto anyone's list.

Do the Cosby show and other like-minded television programs have an impact on God's people? Do pictures of life that portray health and wholeness without any need for God discourage Christians from actively witnessing about Jesus and the purpose of his death? I contend that the answer is yes. We are influenced by our environments. Input from our culture massages our minds. The dominant forces of self-sufficiency and secularization in the culture stand as threats to many committed Christians. They make contemporary believers feel insecure.

Our self-perceptions and how we relate to others are also affected by societal patterns of self-sufficiency and secularization. The honest desires of many followers of Jesus who would like to engage their friends in discussions about God and his ways are squelched. Many Christian believers become defensive. Instead of speaking out they remain silent. Instead of reaching out they turn inward to themselves and their Christian communities. Too frequently, the result is intimidation.

The Minority Shift
Another intimidating force in the culture is the dawning realization that committed Christians are becoming North American minorities.

The secularized segment of society is growing. According to studies by James Engel and others, in 1950 in the U.S.A. it was estimated that 15% of the society was unchurched and secular. By 1985 the secular society had doubled to approximately 38%.[7]

A 1985 U.S.A. Gallup poll reveals society's perception of God and religion. While 95% of the population believe in God and 80% embrace the divinity of Jesus, only a minority of 40% express their beliefs through consistent church attendance. When asked to name the four gospels, only 46% knew about Matthew, Mark, Luke and John. Although 72% claim to accept the Bible as the Word of God, only 15% claim to read it on a daily basis; 24% say they never open the book.[8]

The Canadian profile is similar. Eighty-three per cent affirm their belief in God; 79% assert that Jesus is the divine son of God. But when asked about "commitment to Christianity," only 44% respond positively.[9]

Psychologically, many of today's serious Christians are experiencing the impact of social demotion. If life in the culture is like the National Football League season, then in the old days it was the committed Christians who repeatedly won the Super Bowl. Certainly, today's Christians are still playing in the league but they seldom make the play-offs. Modern believers have been robbed of their former status and popularity. Instead of playing on the favorite teams in the nation, today's followers of Jesus face the prospect of suffering through consecutive losing seasons.

Committed Christians should lament this shift in their status. Spiritual decline in a society should always trigger sorrow—and even fear. A democratic society void of Christian principles is vulnerable to the vices of the powerful. For many reasons, being in the majority is the preferred position. Being able to use strength for the collective good of a culture is a great privilege. Suffering from intimidation is less likely when you can carry the vote. The entrenchment of secularism as a viable alternative for life ought to trouble serious followers of Jesus. Everyone loses when God is set aside.

Yet there are still many reasons why Christians should take heart. God is committed to working with members of minority groups. Caleb and Joshua stand as a reminder of where the real power rests. In the end, God's plan for that segment of history in his universe did unfold. The giants were put in their place, and the people of Israel took the land and entered Canaan.

As today's committed Christians are given eyes to see and the faith to boldly implement God's vision for the future of their land, God's plan for these times will unfold also.

ENGAGING PLURALISM

BUYING AN ICE CREAM CONE USED TO BE SIMPLE. NOW it's complex. In the old days, when we were a vanilla, chocolate and strawberry society, the decision at the ice cream counter was easy. Today it's Baskin and Robbins with 31 different flavors. Is it going to be another Pralines 'n' Cream or shall we try a new taste experience? Shall we go for the feature of the day or the latest flavor to climb on the selection chart? When we finally make up our minds, the salesperson asks, "Will that be a regular or sugar cone or would you like to try our new waffle variety? Would you like a small, medium or large?" By this time, the easier response is, "You decide, let me just pay for it and eat it."

We live in an age when we can decide to go a movie and make our selection after we get there. What do we want tonight? Will it be romance, a war story, a horror film, a little sex or a lot of sex, a little violence or a lot of violence, a detective plot, something that deals with an issue, a suspense thriller, an academy-award winner, or an acclaimed low-budget production? The modern cineplex caters to the temperament of our multioption culture.

A Pluralistic Society

The complexity of life is not limited to purchasing an afternoon treat at the ice cream counter or deciding what to do for an evening's entertainment. Moral decisions, ethical dilemmas, lifestyle options—they are now areas where we must make a myriad of decisions. The culture no longer hands down an accepted set of rules for how to live or provides a single standard for judging right and wrong.

We live in a *pluralistic society*. In simple terms, *plural* means "more than one." When applied to beliefs or systems of thought, to be pluralistic is to acknowledge more than one ultimate principle. In a pluralistic society, various points of view are encouraged and considered valid.

The emergence of a pluralistic culture has serious consequences for determining what are acceptable methods of evangelism. Confrontational styles of witnessing were never popular, but today they are considered offensive. The claim that there was only one way to God was at least marketable in the past, but in today's milieu it is repulsive. Some people would like to turn back the cultural clock. But going back is not an option. Engaging pluralism with a full awareness of how the informal laws of life work in this age is the better alternative.

The religious profile of North America used to be monolithic. Increased ethnicity, the arrival of representatives from other world religions and experimentation with other supernatural alternatives, such as the New Age movement, are altering our religious profile.

At this stage in North American history, our culture is a hybrid of our past and present. The strong Christian legacy from the past remains influential. Consequently, the majority still believes in God. He is there as an accepted reference point. But as the Christian dominance declines in the culture, God exists more as an *impersonal idea* than as a personal force. People are still Christian theists, but many live like practical atheists. God is not dead but he is a casualty of indifference. The majority of people are not mad at God—they are indifferent. They are not carrying God-grudges around on their shoulders. Rather, they are passive and polite about him. They continue to vote for God's existence in the same way they believe in motherhood and good government.

The strong hold of Christianity on the culture has been broken. Other ideologies have established their presence. The forces of secularism, materialism, hedonism and various forms of humanism have legitimized their existence. The society is genuinely pluralistic. Many ways to believe and behave have received the official "Good Housekeeping" seal of approval. Christianity is but one voice among other voices calling for allegiance.

Religious pluralism in a country complicates life and can create tensions. The societal and interpersonal challenge that emerges when religious pluralism prevails is *How can we learn to respect each other's beliefs and live with each other's differences?*

Tolerance—The New Golden Rule

Permissiveness is the attitude that controls a pluralistic culture. The posture of permissiveness is expressed in dispositions that say, "I'll do my thing and you do your thing." "Don't push your views on me and I won't push mine on you." "Go ahead, express your freedom. Just let me express mine too."

In practice, the social code says, "Live and let live." If you want the freedom to preach about Jesus, you must also allow others to preach against him. If you want to articulate an antiabortionist (pro-life) position, you must give others the right to champion an abortionist (pro-choice) point of view. If you think apartheid is wrong and want to press for economic sanctions, then in a pluralistic society you implicitly give permission for the opposite perspective to be represented too.

Tolerance is the golden rule of pluralism. "Do unto others as you would have them do unto you" gets changed to "Let others do what they want to do so you can do what you want to do."

In a pluralistic society, a judgmental spirit breaks the social code. Morality is a private matter. Values are sorted according to individual tastes. "Value systems embodied in styles of living are not right or wrong, true or false. They are matters of personal choice. The operative principle is . . . respect for the freedom of each person to choose the values that he or she will live by."[1] Personal ethics, then, have an elastic quality about them. They can be stretched. One is within bounds as long as one's conduct does not transgress prevailing social standards or violate the criminal code.

One paradox remains with modern pluralism. Although tolerance is the acclaimed golden rule, the one thing that is not tolerated is intolerance. Allan Bloom, in *The Closing of the American Mind*, reveals this incongruity: "It is open to all kinds of men, all kinds of life-styles, all ideologies. There is no enemy other than the man who is not open to everything."[2]

In a pluralistic society, however, people who assert that truth exists push the tolerance code too far. Claiming that life begins at conception is too unilateral for pro-abortionists to handle, even though the belief they hold is the opposite extreme. Decreeing that homosexual relations are wrong is too harsh for the pluralist. Pressing the point that there is only one way to God goes too far. The claim is too certain, too black and white to be accepted. Pluralism is an open system but not without some restraints and inconsistencies. In order to understand how pluralism works in our age and to interact within it, we must grant its practitioners the right to their premises and relate to them with grace.

Mandatory Choices

Ice cream counters and cineplexes all make the same announcement. Choices are mandatory in a pluralistic society. Having alternatives gives pluralism its identity. Making choices and having the prerogative to decide symbolize the pluralistic way of life. One-way thinking belongs to another age. From the pluralistic point of view, restricting oneself to a "one way" mentality is like going to a library and always reading the same book. Whether lifestyles or politics are the issue, allowing for personal differences is the pluralistic way.

John Stott asks the timely question, "Should Christians attempt to impose their views on a largely non-Christian nation?" He then goes on to observe that the two most common responses to the dilemma is represented by opposite extremes. "One is 'imposition,' the crusading attempt to coerce people by legislation to accept the Christian way. The other is 'laissez-faire,' the defeatist decision to leave people alone in their non-Christian ways, and not interfere or try to influence them in any way."[3]

Opting for either of these extremes—imposition or laissez-faire noninvolvement—is hardly the biblical way. Simply lamenting the situation is also an inadequate response. Christians and those who believe otherwise must figure out how to live with the social realities of both religious and cultural pluralism. In the society we have fashioned, we must learn to respect each other's beliefs and figure out how to live peaceably with each other's differences.

A good model for how we relate to those who are different from us is to reflect on how God relates to us. When we consider carefully our own experiences with God, we realize that he has not been coercive with us. He is long-suffering and does not revert to any pressure tactics. He is patient with us. Certainly Jesus was careful not to exploit people when he was recruiting his followers. Throughout the Gospels we have no record of his begging people to join his team or pressuring people to conform to his ways. In fact, Jesus tended toward the other extreme. Instead of cajoling people to believe and follow, he even gave his disciples openings to leave (Jn 6:60-69).

On the other hand, we have images of God as a jealous lover. His enduring commitment to woo the Israelites is undeniable. He didn't just casually say, "Choose you this day whom you will serve" and then back away. God kept returning through the voice of his prophets, offering second and third chances to respond. Then there is God's boldest move in history. Sending Jesus to win back the allegiance of his creation is the most compelling of all his initiatives. When we think about the cross, there is nothing innocent or lighthearted about God's desire to call his people back to himself.

If we let God's record in history and his treatment of us be the guide for how we should treat others, we see that strong initiative must be taken to win the day. A game plan for influencing our pluralistic society with the enduring message of the gospel is necessary.

Accept, Appreciate, Influence

There is always more than one way to meet a challenge. And it is possible to design more than one strategy to convey the gospel in a culture. Earlier we looked at Jesus' interaction with Zacchaeus and his pattern of *praying, caring* and *communicating*. This strategy is the basis for all of our discipleship. Now we need a paradigm for dealing with pluralism specifically.

We can find that paradigm when we observe the apostle Paul's encounter with the Athenians on Mars Hill (Acts 17:16-34). Here Paul provides a model for how we can engage people to consider the gospel in our pluralistic society.

Paul is alone in the city of Athens. He is waiting for Silas and Timothy to join him but he is not in the mood to waste time. He goes for a walk through that great city and comes back "greatly distressed" (v. 16). His spirit is troubled by all the false idols. He knows they are symbols of belief that cannot meet the needs of the Athenians who worship them.

Paul starts talking to people around him. Specifically, he goes to where he knows he will find religious people. He reasons with the "Jews and God-fearing Greeks" who are there (v. 17). He doesn't limit his discussions to just the religious types in Athens, however. Day after day he talks with people who just "happen to be" in the marketplace (v. 17). He engages in debate with "a group of Epicurean and Stoic philosophers" (v. 18). The ideas Paul communicates are new to their minds. The philosophers are known for both their pleasure-seeking and their fatalism. Paul unsettles them with talk about "Jesus and the resurrection" (v. 18). They are intrigued. They want clarification (v. 19). Since they have time on their hands (v. 21), they invite Paul to join them for a formal session in their chambers. Paul is pleased and he accepts the invitation. They walk up the hill together.

Ajith Fernando from Sri Lanka observes that in this situation "we see a twofold attitude of Paul to other religions. On the one hand there is a firm belief in the wrongness of life apart from Christ. On the other hand there is a respect for all individuals because they are intelligent human beings endowed by God with the privilege and responsibility of choosing to accept or reject the gospel."[4]

Accept People

I would propose that Paul's attitude of respect toward others freed him to genuinely *accept* the Athenian philosophers even though he did not agree with them. In doing so, Paul demonstrates how to open doors in order to witness effectively in our pluralistic society. If Paul had postured an attitude of judgment or superiority toward the philosophers, they would have written off both Paul and his message. By meeting them on their terms with an open attitude, Paul communicates his acceptance of them and opens doors to potential influence.

Many Christians have reservations about accepting people who are not Christians. Legitimate questions can be raised around the issue of Christians extending open arms to those who have rejected the claims of Christ. Will my acceptance be misinterpreted as an endorsement? Will acceptance of non-Christians soften some of my own convictions? Will my acceptance get confused with approval and agreement? What will my fellow Christians think? I know I'm not supposed to judge people, but is simply accepting people as they are going too far toward the other extreme?

One way to quell these concerns is to see the consequences of closing ourselves off from interaction with non-Christians. When we are unaccepting, we communicate many negative signals:

"Christians think they're superior to everyone."

"I get the feeling I am being judged around them."

"They must feel like they are better, certainly more righteous."

"What I really think is that many Christians are insecure and have strong feelings of inferiority. It looks to me like Christians are afraid and have to protect themselves by keeping their distance from people who think differently from their own kind."

Another reason for questioning our reticence is to realize that *acceptance is not approval*. When a non-Christian receives full and unqualified acceptance from a Christian, it is not the same as approving everything about that person. Just as God loves the sinner but detests the sin, so the Christian is called to accept the unbeliever without confusing who a person is with what a person does.

Also, *acceptance does not compromise our spiritual convictions*. When Christians relate to non-Christians without judging them, they should see that they are extending dignity to people in the process of building significant relationships. Obviously, the potential of the non-Christian becoming a negative spiritual influence on the Christian is a risk. Certainly, followers of Jesus need to live with guarded wisdom, but living with high acceptance levels of the unspiritual has nothing inherently in common with spiritual compromise.

The practice of acceptance sets up a reciprocal law of life. In interpersonal relationships, if you don't give it, you don't get it. If you do not accept people, they do not accept you. If you do not listen seriously to people, they do not listen seriously to you. Honest "dialogue requires the free interchange of ideas between two people who are both full-fledged

speakers and full-fledged listeners."[5] Unless you extend a nonjudg-
mental attitude toward people in a pluralistic society, you push them
away from the range of your influence. Lack of acceptance precludes
the potential of getting close enough to effectively share God's good
news with people.

For the Christian who extends acceptance to non-Christians, something else happens. *When you accept someone, he or she is no longer a threat
to you.* Just as "love drives out fear," acceptance disarms intimidation
(1 Jn 4:18). Acceptance changes the dynamics of relationships. Acceptance sends messages like, "I'm not setting myself up as the judge
of your life and neither am I trying to impose my conclusions on you."
As a result, people are encouraged to respond in the same manner.
Acceptance fosters acceptance, and both parties in the relationship are freed to be who they are without being threatened by each
other.

In the introduction to his book *The Different Drum,* Scott Peck articulates how acceptance should work:

> I must write, therefore, out of the particularity of my culture as a
> citizen of the United States and my faith as a Christian. Should
> some take offense at this, I ask them to remember that it is their
> responsibility to embrace my particularity, my uniqueness, just as
> it is my responsibility to embrace theirs.[6]

The lack of acceptance by Christians of those who are not yet followers of Jesus is one of the major obstacles to fruitful witnessing. Failure
on the part of Christians to extend acceptance to nonbelievers shuts
down relationships before they have an opportunity to develop. The
wrong signal is sent and the door is shut.

Raising our acceptance levels of people who believe other things
about God and life is essential in order to witness effectively in our
pluralistic culture. However, simply accepting non-Christians is not
going far enough. Taking the next step to genuinely appreciate people who are not professing Christians will both enhance life on earth
and help them move into God's eternal kingdom.

Appreciate People

Paul is our model again. Although he has an agenda that is important to him, Paul does not ignore what is important to others. In the Athens situation, Paul's beginning is brilliant. With obvious inspiration from the Spirit of Christ, Paul acknowledges the religious realities of his audience. "Men of Athens!" he begins, "I see that in every way you are very religious. For as I walked around and looked carefully at your objects of worship, I even found an altar with this inscription: TO AN UNKNOWN GOD. Now what you worship as something unknown I am going to proclaim to you" (Acts 17:22-23).

There is no hint of attack or aggressiveness in Paul's approach. His aim is to build on what exists and bring clarity to what is unknown. His temperament is not to tear down or demean in any way.

After his introduction Paul moves to the meat of his message. He ascribes to the unknown god the credentials of his Father in heaven. He is the one "who made the world." He doesn't live in human temples; he is too great to have any needs; and he is the one who has determined where everyone he has created should live (vv. 24-27).

Then Paul demonstrates another moment of genius. Rather than quoting from the Old Testament, his common practice when his audience included Jews, Paul quotes from his listeners' teachers. Showing appreciation for what is valued by the philosophers themselves, Paul continues, " 'For in him we live and move and have our being.' As some of your own poets have said, 'We are his offspring' " (v. 28).

New Testament scholar F. F. Bruce explains that the first quotation, "For in him we live and move and have our being," has been attributed to Epidenides the Cretan.[7] The statement underscores everyone's dependence on God for existence. The second expression, "We are his offspring," reinforces the same message. It is from a poem by Aratus about the supreme being of Stoic philosophy.

By acknowledging the existence of the altar to the "unknown god," Paul states a fact of life in Athens and at the same time builds a bridge with his audience. By quoting the poets of his listeners, Paul affirms their status as good teachers. He appreciates and validates the truth they are teaching. The relational distance closes. There is bonding between the speaker and the listener. Appreciation by the communicator of what is valued by the audience draws them together.

Just as many Christians are reticent to extend acceptance to non-Christians, others struggle to genuinely appreciate the beauty and good in those who do not overtly acknowledge God. Even though it is impossible to deny the good that is present in non-Christians, it is not always easy for Christians to affirm the good that is there.

Your doorbell rings, and when you open it Gwen greets you with a smile and asks, "Would you like to make a donation to the United Way appeal again this year?" Gwen lives four doors down the street and you know she never darkens the door of a church. You are impressed with her manner and her desire to help in the community.

It's "parent's night" at your local school. You have heard a few things about your daughter's teacher but you've never met him. As you talk during the interview, you sense genuine concern from the teacher for your daughter. You also know he is not a Christian. On the way home you think about his cordial manner and obvious commitment to his students—including your daughter. Although you wish he were a believer, you are nonetheless grateful for him.

You are vacationing with your wife and, by the time you check in at the airline counter, there are only single seats left—all in the center. You don't travel together very often and are irritated that you cannot sit close enough to talk. Being crammed in the center seat is also something you try to avoid. You find your wife's seat and head for your own assignment toward the back of the plane. Just as you are getting settled and continuing to complain under your breath, the man on the aisle next to your wife comes back and offers to change seats with you. You explain that you have the undesirable center seat. He acknowledges that he doesn't like them either but knows you would like to join your wife. You accept his graciousness with an enthusiastic "thank you."

Later in the flight you go back to again express your appreciation for his thoughtfulness. He has been drinking too much and his language is foul. You go back to your seat musing about the good and the distasteful in him. You think about your own foul attitude about sitting alone, and center seats, and know you have a dark side too. You reflect on your claim to be a committed Christian and wonder if you would have given up your seat on the aisle if you had been in his place. You think about the good in people who seem to be disconnected from your God.

There are strong reasons to celebrate and affirm the good in those who make no claim to know Christ. Speaking in the context of relating to those who embrace other world religions, Ajith Fernando reasons, "It is because we believe in the supremacy of Christ that we are not afraid to affirm what is good in other faiths."[8]

The teachings of the world's religions are not all wrong. They convey part of what God has decreed and established to be right and true. In Christ and his teachings, however, we have the fullest disclosure of God's revelation and truth. His person and his teachings are authoritative truth. When other claims are put forth, they are to be tested against Christ's standards. If there is no conflict, we can agree and be supportive. If there is conflict, we bow to Christ's Word and reject what counters his claims. Paul was free to cite the philosopher's poets because he knew their teachings were consistent with Christ's teachings. He knew that all truth was God's truth regardless of who was saying it.

Not only is all truth from God, but all good is from God. When nonchristians collect funds to respond to needs in their community; when teachers care for students; when thoughtfulness prompts a stranger to give up his preferred seat; whenever good is expressed in this world, God is at work. Whether or not people acknowledge him or are aware of him, God is the source of all good. Regardless of how sinful and broken people become, they are still left with God's "beauty marks" showing through. The image of God is etched so deeply into his creation that it is impossible to completely obliterate his likeness. Theologians refer to "prevenient" or "common grace" when identifying the good that rests in every person. To believe otherwise is to be victimized by heretical teaching.

The teaching of Genesis 1 is that we are created with the capacity to reflect the likeness of God. Certainly, the arrival and certainty of sin is disastrous. The power of sin attacks the beauty of the image of God in his creation. Every person sins and comes short of the glory of God (Rom 3:23). The potential of every human person to reign down evil on individuals and society is shocking. But as potent and destructive as sin can be, the image of God cannot be totally wiped out. There is always beauty left. The image of the Creator cannot be completely removed from people any more than our hearts can be removed and still be alive. And that is why we are mandated to appreciate the good in people whether or not they claim to know and serve God. We celebrate the good in people because God is the source of all good, whenever and wherever it is expressed.

Christians have the truth about life. God's people know why there is light and why there is darkness, why there is good and evil. Followers of Jesus have the inside story on why both virtue and horror flow from the human heart. They know that their only claim to potential good is because of how God has designed them. They know the good news that Christ has come to deal with the dark side of the human heart.

Knowing the truth about life and convincing others to believe it are two separate matters. And the reality in this age is that Christ's good news is not being believed by the majority. In response, if Christians will both accept and appreciate the people in their lives who have not received Christ, they will be in a position to present God's claims with positive force. A few months after participating in an evangelistic training session, one participant wrote to affirm the theory in his experience:

I just wanted to tell you that I am already seeing good things coming out of the practice of valuing nonbeliever's viewpoints. In my office, I have always had more success witnessing to Orthodox Jews and Muslims than to the public at large. I now realize that I have always respected the values of the Jews and Muslims, but not of others. This attitude must have come across even though it was not conscious. My valuing every person's point of view has made them more open to me and the gospel.

When *acceptance* is the attitude and when *appreciation* for what is good in people is expressed, followers of Jesus are in a position to *influence* those who have not yet accepted Christ and his teachings. The paradigm is not offered as a technique to control or to be deceptive with people. Neither should the approach be viewed as a procedure or simple method. Rather, the paradigm is offered as a lifestyle that has integrity for those who call themselves committed Christians. It is a framework for responding to the people God brings into their lives.

Influence People

By its very nature, a pluralistic society is open to new influences. As soon as a society endorses a "multiplicity" of options rather than pouring life into a "one way" mold, an open system is created. In contrast to a closed system that resists the introduction of anything new, an open system welcomes what has not yet been discovered or experienced.

The people of Athens lived in an open system too. The Acts account says they "spent their time . . . talking about and listening to the latest ideas" (Acts 17:21). Like ancient Athens, our culture is hooked on whatever is the "latest"—whether it be ideas, news, technology, fashion, entertainment, automobiles, travel and so on. There is even interest in what is the latest in spiritual experiences. Be certain that any society that is looking for what's new is also an open system and subject to being influenced.

The challenge for the serious Christian is to live in our pluralistic open system and be convinced that it can be influenced. Too often

Christians live with fear of the world. They are convinced that rather than being an influence, they will be influenced. The world appears to be stronger. Their status as members of a minority group leaves them threatened by the majority.

But when followers of Jesus walk into their world of relationships with identities that include "I am an influence for God and good," then the world will have to take Christ seriously.

When Paul addressed the men of Athens, he was there to influence them to consider Christ and accept his claims on their lives. Paul's intentions were clear in his mind before he reached the outskirts of Athens. His agenda was established long before his invitation to speak. Whether he was reasoning in the synagogue, interacting in the marketplace or making his formal presentation, Paul's behavior was highly intentional. When it came time to address his audience on Mars Hill, Paul was not just delivering information in a lecture. As he connected with his audience and referenced the "unknown God," as he endowed his heavenly Father with his credentials and cited the philosopher's poets, Paul was committed to lifting up Christ and the reality of his resurrection. Paul's mind was clear and his message was precise. He wanted his listeners to believe in his Lord.

And some members of the audience *did* believe. A few were intrigued enough to say, "We want to hear you again." Then there were others who thought the resurrection was nonsense. They sneered at the idea and flatly rejected Christ as an option for their lives and allegiance (Acts 17:32-33).

People continue to make the same responses to Jesus and the claim of his resurrection today. Some people look at Christianity and Christ and are unable to make a clear decision. They need space and time and more input about what it all means. Others are more categorical. On the one hand, some are able to place their faith and confidence in Christ. On the other hand, others are definitive about saying no. They end up going somewhere else with their interests and loyalties.

Win-Win Witnessing

Paul's stance of accepting people, genuinely appreciating who they are, and then influencing them to consider Christ is a win-win approach to witnessing.

Those who witness in this manner win. They are able to relate to people and enjoy them for who they are. They are released from any tendency to judge those in their presence. Signals of superiority are shut down. Yet they are given a definitive game plan to communicate the gospel in a way that frees them to firmly hold to their own faith without being defensive.

Those who are recipients of this approach to witnessing win too. They receive signals that tell them they have every right to be what they are. They sense they are respected. Yet they are challenged to think, to deal honestly with themselves, to rechart their lives and become more than they are. They are asked to risk a life-transforming encounter with the God who created them and desires to redeem them.

In a pluralistic society, people have a wide range of legitimate choices when it comes to deciding what they will believe and how they want to behave. God's strategy is to use his committed people to influence others to consider Christ as a viable alternative in these times. Christians who open their arms of *acceptance* and express *appreciation* toward the non-Christians in their lives will be used by God to *influence* others to accept Christ in this age.

Chapter Five

DECODING CULTURAL CHRISTIANITY

GOD USED TO BE OUR HERO, THE STAR PLAYER IN THE starting line-up. Today, we have relegated him to the reserves. He sits on the bench as a second stringer. It is only in certain circumstances that he is brought off the bench to enter the game.

In the eyes of our culture, God is still on the team but gets limited play time. In Canada when young adults aged 15-24 were asked about their religious inclinations and commitments, several matters became clear.[1] Like American young people, Canadian youth are still identifying with religious organizations. Seventy-seven per cent call themselves Protestants or Catholics. An additional 3% identify with one of the other world religions or the Jewish tradition. Thus a total of 80% raise their hands and say, "I am a religious something."[2]

By contrast, only 17% attend church regularly; 16% contend it is important to live out their faith in everyday life; 14% highly value religion; 12% claim God has a great deal of influence on their lives; and a meager 3% of the 15- to 24-year-olds acknowledge that religious leaders strongly influence their lives. The evidence speaks loudly. Only a small minority are serious about their religious commitment.

But when it comes to using the services of the church for the cherished rites of passage in life, a clear majority of those same young people expect to utilize the privileges of religious rites. Specifically, 82% expect to get married in a church or synagogue, and 85% anticipate having a minister, priest or rabbi to officiate at their funerals.

How did it happen? What is the explanation for the user-friendly attitude that prevails toward religion—while at the same time, a serious spiritual commitment is considered to be unimportant by so many? Why the religious dualism?

Cultural Christians

Christianity and North American culture are inseparable. Like mixing together different kinds of coffee beans and then passing them through a grinder, Christianity and culture have been blended together. Separation of church and state may be an operational premise for the courts to ponder, but the fact remains that life in North America cannot be understood without computing the pervasive influence of the Christian faith. The historical decision to inscribe "In God We Trust" on American currency is a graphic symbol of the blend. The paradox of linking God and money makes a statement about the ambiguity that prevails. Separating Christians from the culture and the culture from Christians may be more difficult than ungrinding the coffee beans.

Difficult or not, if there is a commitment to effectively engage the culture with a credible gospel, then we must be sure to sort out what is Christian and what is cultural.

In both the United States and Canada, eight out of ten people affirm the belief that "Jesus was the divine Son of God." The vote of confidence in Jesus is impressive, but the more intriguing issue revolves around what the claim really means. What are the religious implications for a society when a strong majority of a population identifies Jesus as divine? How does this evident openness to God affect evangelism in the culture?

One way to view the eight out of ten who make the belief claim in Jesus is to see them in two categories: *culturalized Christians* and *those who have personally encountered Christ.* Those in the first group have been socialized to be religious people. They have a Christian orientation and identity. People in the other category have had some bona fide personalization of their faith in Jesus.

A more specific way to think about this religious consensus around Jesus is to reason that almost everyone in the Western world has an individual view of him. They may not be able to consciously articulate what they think about Jesus, but they do have a favorable disposition toward him.

For example, some view Jesus as a good *Teacher*. They simply affirm him as someone who has good ideas. These people have heard that Jesus is a good moral teacher and they basically accept that claim. Consequently, he deserves to be listened to and to be taken somewhat seriously.

Others acknowledge that Jesus is a *Model* for human behavior. They are attracted to him and have inclinations or even aspirations to be like him.

These first two orientations toward Jesus can be seen as the building blocks for creating a cultural Christianity. Jesus is acknowledged and given some authoritative status.

Those who move beyond seeing Jesus in just cultural terms lift him up as *Savior*. To them, Jesus is the long-promised Messiah, the Son of God who came to earth to take the sin of the world on himself. This

sector of society concludes that what Jesus did on the cross has implications for their personal salvation and eternal destiny.

Still others have an even higher view of Jesus. They contend that
to really give Jesus the place he deserves, he must be accepted as *Lord.*
Their drive is to obey him. They rise in the morning with the attitude
that says, "Jesus, show me, tell me what to do, and I will give myself
to do it."

The entrenchment of Christianity in the culture results in everyone
having some familiarity with Jesus. Even if he does not reach the
minimal status of being a teacher, at the very least *Jesus* is a common,
everyday swear word. The tendency then is for people in the society
to access Jesus at their particular reference point. Jesus may be nothing more than an object of profanity. Then again, he may carry the
status of Teacher, Model, Savior or Lord.

Religious-cultural events during the calendar year reinforce the
existing status of Jesus that people carry in their minds. Every Christmas, almost everyone in society walks into shopping centers and buys
presents with "Joy to the world, the Lord has come" playing in the
background. Annually each Easter, a civic holiday commemorates the
death and resurrection of Jesus. The risen Christ gets extraordinary
attention.

Evaluating the Marriage

The repeated interplay between culture and religion has numerous
implications for evangelism. There are both positive and negative
effects.

On the positive side, Jesus is a reference point for communication.
He gets airtime. It happened when hockey star Wayne Gretzky was
traded from the Edmonton Oilers to the Los Angeles Kings. A sports
commentator was asked if he thought acquiring the "great one" would
turn the Kings into a serious contender to win the Stanley Cup. Desiring to be a little profound, the commentator reflected for a moment
and responded, "With all due respect, if Jesus Christ played for the

Los Angeles Kings, they would not be a threat to win it all."

Our Christian heritage and acceptance of Jesus' teachings lifts our overall quality of life. For example, honesty is affirmed as an important value.[3] A few months ago I was having a hamburger in an intriguing restaurant called "The Cultural Cow." I noticed two young men enjoying themselves over their meal, which included a couple of beers. They finished their time together and paid their bill at the cashier. Within two or three minutes they returned to speak to the person who had taken their money. They told the man, "As we got out onto the street we looked at each other and said, 'That was sure cheap. I wonder if they charged us enough.' We think you missed the beers."

The young men were right and they dug back into their pockets. But the question is, What prompts young men to return to the cash register to pay for their beers? People are honest because our Christian heritage instilled that particular value in them. The influence of Jesus' teachings are still with us.

On the negative side, Christian leaders with noble aspirations to evangelize can misread how people respond to the claims of Christ. Positive predispositions toward Jesus can get confused with genuine experiences of conversion.

Young people are particularly susceptible to the phenomenon. It can happen when a Christian athlete is given airtime at a high-school assembly. He walks on stage to the microphone as a hero in the eyes of at least some of the beholders. His intentions are honorable. His experience in Christ is genuine. He talks about life on the playing field and in the locker room. He shares his testimony in a sensitive and humorous manner. He describes how God has changed his life and gives him strength. In a direct and caring way he goes on to call his listeners to believe in Jesus and follow him too. Prepared response cards are distributed. The teen-agers are asked to make their private decisions.

The young people look at the cards carefully. The procedure is a serious matter for them. They read the questions: *Do you believe that Jesus is the Son of God who died for your sins? Do you want to receive Christ as your personal savior?*

There are little square boxes on the cards for people to mark their *x*'s as an indication of their decision. They are also asked to write in their names and telephone numbers so someone from the sponsoring group can contact them to confirm their commitment and help them grow in Christ. A significant percentage of the audience mark their *x*'s in the boxes. The cards are collected. A count is tallied. The organizers celebrate.

The people assigned to the task of follow-up frequently tell a different story. Of the scores who indicated their commitment to believe, only a few are prepared to talk on the telephone about their decision. Even fewer are open to the possibility of meeting to discuss their new faith in Jesus. One or two of the respondents may accept an invitation to study the Bible in a small group.

What transpires during the few days between the well-intended decision to become a Christian and the time when follow-up contact is made? Did anything happen that had spiritual significance as the *x*'s were being marked?

Only God knows for sure, but some projections can be made. Assuredly, some young people do meet Jesus in those situations. They become new creatures in Christ and follow him for a lifetime, but they are typically a very small minority of those who mark the boxes. In the case of most who mark their *x*'s, however, the experience is less consequential. Some young people simply overidentify with the athlete. They would like to be like their hero. For others, the questions on the card connect with their cultural predisposition to be open to Jesus' claims. They simply respond accordingly. "Of course, Jesus is the divine Son of God. Everyone knows that!" In other instances, the young people are just casting their vote in favor of the whole event. For them, it's another experience, valid for the moment but without long-term implications.

Regardless of people's age, cultural familiarity with Christian truth both confuses communication and dulls spiritual interest. When people hear words and ideas they have heard before, they assume they know what is meant. As people receive information that activates past impressions, prior understanding blocks the pathway to new meanings.

Converting Cultural Christians

The incessant marketing of Jesus and Christianity on radio and television has had a general numbing affect on many young adults and older people. The very sound of a preacher's voice is a stimulus to think, "I've heard all that before" and to keep turning the dial or flipping the channels. Decades of repetitious religious input has created familiarity, but it has not produced spiritual commitment. The phenomena has helped push God to the sidelines of the culture.

Consequently, injecting fresh meaning into the belief claim that "Jesus is the divine Son of God" is a complex matter. For many in North America, familiarity with Jesus and language about him stands in the way of a deeper spiritual experience with him. In their self-perceptions, most people in the society already believe in Jesus. Therefore, culturally defined, they are Christians. And they are dubious about the Christian faith being more than what they are already experiencing. Until they are prompted to take a fresh look at Jesus or until they see convincing evidence that Christianity is more than what they already know, God will remain dormant in their daily lives.

The onus to overcome the consequences of the blurring of culture and Christianity is clearly on the shoulders of those who desire to communicate the full meaning of Jesus' life and death. Understanding the perceptions of the audience is the responsibility of the speaker—not the listener.

Showing All of Christ

Bringing clarity about who Jesus is has always been the central issue in evangelism, and until Jesus returns a second time, it needs to continue to be so.

The situation was no different for Jesus himself. Early in his ministry, when Jesus returned to Nazareth with his disciples, people in his hometown were captivated by his teaching but they were unable to change their first impressions of his identity.

"Isn't this the carpenter? Isn't this Mary's son and the brother of James, Joseph, Judas and Simon? Aren't his sisters here with us?" (Mk 6:3). The biblical record shows that the citizens of Nazareth "took offense" at Jesus, and Jesus was frustrated that in his hometown "a prophet [was] without honor" and he could not do any miracles there (Mk 6:1-6).

Jesus frequently created debate around his own identity. He called for people to decide to be for him or against him based on who they perceived him to be. Jesus deliberately triggered controversy with the claims he made about himself.

"I am the light of the world" (Jn 8:12).

"If you knew me, you would know my Father also" (Jn 8:19).

"I am the good shepherd" (Jn 10:11).

"I am the true vine" (Jn 15:1).

"I am the way and the truth and the life" (Jn 14:6).

In the final hours of his life on this earth, as Jesus was on trial before the Sanhedrin, the verdict revolved around the issue that was most threatening and would not go away.

The chief priest said to him, "I charge you under oath by the living God: Tell us if you are the Christ, the Son of God." Jesus replied, "Yes, it is as you say" (Mt 26:63-64).

What are the implications in today's world where eight out of ten people claim they believe that Jesus is the divine Son of God?

Surely the first step is to remember that people, whatever their backgrounds, have some culturally inherited views about Jesus. The next move is to simply accept people and what they claim to believe about him. Once those steps have been taken, then it will be critical to find out what people mean when they say, "I believe that Jesus is divine."

When it comes to our attitudes, it will be important to surrender unilateral thinking that either labels people as "believers" or "unbelievers." Implicit in the temperament to slot people in one category or the other is to imply that they either believe in Jesus or don't believe in him, that they have accepted Jesus or rejected him. Human experience in a society with an abundance of Christian reference points is not that clear-cut.

Rather, when relating to people, the more central issue is to connect with them where they are. We begin by focusing on how they view Jesus. Is their view a scaled-down, cultural conception of Jesus as Teacher or Model? Or is it genuinely Christian? Perhaps they have already looked seriously at Jesus as a potential Savior and rejected him.

Because of our Christian heritage, becoming a true believer for many people will first involve lifting the level of how they view Jesus. Once they see him in his full stature, they can deal with the implications of their new understanding. Then they will be in a position to join with the apostle Peter and declare, "Lord, to whom shall we go? You have the words of eternal life. We believe and know that you are the Holy One of God" (Jn 6:68-69).

God's people who effectively engage a culture that has a Christian heritage will need to be students of both the Bible and the culture itself. The general populace in society who have inherited a view of Jesus need understanding and sensitivity more than they need another announcement that Jesus died to save them from their sins. They need to be taken seriously, invited to process their spiritual convictions and helped to unsort their cultural religion from their personal need to encounter Christ. And to meet that challenge, we cannot afford to have a small view of God.

Getting the Big Picture

God's revelation extends back to the beginning of time; it details the historical roots for a modern faith; it speaks to both personal and corporate ethics; it offers a framework for values; it articulates guidelines for seeking justice, holy living, lifestyle decisions and resolving conflict. What God has made known provides a basis to speak to current social problems and political concerns, as well as to the need for personal salvation. God's revelation lets us know ahead of time that we will be held accountable for how we live on planet Earth and that his hope for us is that we will live with him forever.

Maintaining a big view of God's revelation introduces positive possibilities for fruitful witnessing. It means the parameters for communicating God's good news are much broader than the content of John 3:16. Although the meaning of "God so loved the world that he gave his only begotten son" is central to the Christian faith, it is not complete. Building on that awareness will bring opportunities to make God's revelation known in ways that are both personal and intriguing.

Everyday, literally around the world, courier companies are delivering paper and packages on behalf of their clients. In God's strategy, his faithful people are the couriers of his good news. Just as courier companies simply deliver what has been given to them, as God's couriers we deliver what God has already given to us. We do not make up the gospel. We deliver it. God is the originator of truth. Our assignment is to communicate God's truth so that it makes sense to those who need to know it.

This understanding makes witnessing more than a robotic procedure. Because God's truth is so multifaceted, whenever we do witness we must choose what part of his revelation to reveal. The art of witnessing is choosing what to put in the package. It is linking the most appropriate dimension of God's truth with the circumstances of the person in the particular situation.

Appeal to Shared Perceptions

During the past several years, God has surprised me with the privilege of putting this theory into practice as a youth consultant. As a result of research and writing in the area of youth and society, I've had the opportunity to interpret the youth culture to educators, parents, community service workers and government officials.

As a professional offering a consulting service to the wider society, my first commitment is to do my best to meet the needs of the client. I clearly understand that fulfilling the terms of the agreement is the first criteria to achieve. If I fail to meet these priorities, regardless of what else happens, I have failed.

As a serious Christian in those situations, however, I also have a personal agenda. I'm anxious to raise some issues that prod people to think about the kind of cultural inheritance we are handing on to the younger generation. What values are we endorsing? In our personal modeling, what lifestyles are we encouraging? My other commitment is to explicitly identify myself as a committed Christian and speak with conviction about some dimension of God's truth for our times.

Part of the presentation usually includes a listing and interpretation of young people's values. For modern youth, values like "friendship, freedom, success and a comfortable life, honesty and forgiveness" all rank near the top. When a comparison is made between young people who attend church regularly and those who do not, with the exceptions of "forgiveness and honesty," there is little difference between the two groups.

However, when "forgiveness" is isolated and analyzed, the findings are significant. While 85% of those who attend church regularly value forgiveness highly, the figure goes down to 58% for those who absent themselves from participation in church life.[4]

Having this information in mind, at some point in the presentation, I often turn to audiences made up of mostly non-Christians and say something like, "Let me speak to you out of my personal biases for a moment. Let's be honest—you have your points of view and I have mine. As a committed Christian, may I make a few comments about what is accompanying the demise of the church in this age? Do you realize what is happening to our society as fewer people attend church and we absorb the decline of religion in our society?"

After spelling out the details of the lower value-orientation toward forgiveness by a growing segment of society who do not attend church, I conclude: "It looks to me that one consequence of increasing secularization and the decline of the church in our times is that we are a culture that is starting to believe that forgiveness is unimportant." Invariably the audience is silenced and pressed into reflection.

After painting a picture of schools, families and workplaces where there is little commitment to seeking forgiveness, the listeners are open to hear the statement: "Life without forgiveness is hell on earth. We need to be careful about what is sneaking in the back door of our changing culture."

Whether people are open to God or not, they quickly compute the consequences of life without forgiveness. Appealing to shared perceptions can open people's eyes to the goodness and wisdom of God's ways. When the ability to forgive is understood as one of God's gifts in Christ, it is a short step to calculate the serious consequences of life without Christ.

There is power in truth when it rings with authenticity. Our challenge is to tell God's unchanging truth more powerfully, more creatively.

Emphasize What's Unique

Another positive way to engage people in today's world who have written off Christianity is to speak to areas of life where secular voices are silent. We can emphasize some dimensions of Christian truth that address questions that people are pressed to think about but seldom talk about.

Followers of Jesus are granted a distinctive perspective on suffering. They can testify that pain does not need to be an end in itself. A more noble character can be its product. The Scriptures speak with directness: "Whenever you face trials . . . you know that the testing of your faith develops perseverance . . . so that you may be mature and complete, not lacking in anything" (Jas 1:2-4). In a realistic way, the Bible even warns God's people not to be surprised "as though something strange were happening to you. But rejoice that you participate in the sufferings of Christ. . . . So then, those who suffer according to God's will should commit themselves to their faithful Creator and continue to do good" (1 Pet 4:12-13, 19). In God's view, suffering is meant to produce something stronger in us, and in some mysterious way, human hurt connects us with the suffering Christ.

Until the day I die I will remember that Saturday morning phone call. The message poured out through broken sobs that Michael and another student had just been killed.

Mike was one of our InterVarsity staff directors. He and a group of students were away on a weekend together when the van in which they were riding collided with a transport truck. The tragedy not only resulted in two deaths, it inflicted other young students with lifelong disabilities. Life is not fair.

Mike was special—bright, gifted, educated and godly. People were drawn to him. He wore his faith in a relaxed but evident manner. He was comfortable relating to the world. It fed his heart for evangelism. His laugh still rings in my ears.

Mike's death still confuses me. And with no satisfactory answers to *why,* my spirit still aches. But I do now what Scripture says; I do know who Jesus is. Over and over the New Testament reveals the compassionate disposition of Jesus. "When he saw the crowds, he had compassion on them, because they were harassed and helpless, like sheep without a shepherd." Jesus again: "I have compassion for these people; they have already been with me three days and have nothing to eat." The Scriptures reveal Jesus' sensitive inner view of life: "He was deeply moved in spirit and troubled . . . Jesus wept" (Mt 9:36, Mk 8:2, Jn 11:33-35). Jesus joins us in our torment. He is empathetic. We are not alone.

Christians who are wrestling with the death of someone dear to them have hope that the world cannot give. Death has been dealt with in the resurrection of Jesus (1 Cor 15). The final word has already been stated.

Sean O'Sullivan still lives a rich life. He has served as both a politician and member of the clergy. His wrestling match with cancer has given him time to contemplate his death. He speaks forcefully from his experience:

> Soon I may be summoned home. But sing no sad songs for me; I am a Christian. Without merit of my own and trusting only in His abundant mercy, I go gently toward that glorious goal. To other cancer victims and their families . . . and all people of goodwill, I say: Remain steadfast, keep stout hearts and hold unwavering hope. Fear not, our God is still at work. However dark the coming days, He will triumph and be with us always, even until the end of time.[5]

Secularism has neither a truthful nor adequate response to suffering or death. Yet at one time or another, everyone is subject to its torment. The gospel, on the other hand, speaks with reality and healing power to those who are hurting and grieving. As Christians, we not only have a message to bear, but we have a presence to bring into the arena of pain. We bring Jesus and we offer ourselves. We bring hope of access to Christ who knows about ultimate suffering and promises to enter into pain with his people. We offer our empathy and practical support by pouring cups of water in the name of Christ.

In a society that prides itself in being self-sufficient, we will be wise to look for the cracks in the culture where human inadequacies still prevail. As Christians respond with sensitive words and appropriate deeds, some in the society will look again at Christ and come to him.

Repackage the Old News

Bringing fresh meaning to ideas people have heard before—particularly if they think they already understand what you are wanting to communicate—is a formidable challenge. But that is exactly the situation facing today's Christians who are committed to making Jesus news again. Frederick Buechner writes:

"I shall go to my grave," a friend of mine once wrote me, "feeling that Christian thought is a dead language—one that feeds many living ones to be sure, one that still sets these vibrating with echoes and undertones, but which I would no more use overtly than I would speak Latin."

I suppose he is right, more right than wrong anyway. If the language that clothes Christianity is not dead, it is, at least for many, dying; and what is really surprising, I suppose, is that it has lasted as long as it has.[6]

Language about God is approaching obsolescence, being relegated to funerals and other official ceremonies that are still deemed necessary.

Some words simply get overused. Christian clichés and the reiteration of religious rhetoric literally drains life out of life-giving ideas. Christian preaching adds to the lament when it is more boring than intriguing. Lack of imagination from preachers, or perhaps it is an inordinate concern to appear orthodox, converts the good news into old news. When you've heard it before, what's the point in listening to it again?

Words get worn down. Like water cutting into a riverbank, words and their meanings suffer the effects of erosion. The word *love* is an example. When *love* is given specific content, it still has no equal. Listen to 1 Corinthians 13: "Love is patient, love is kind. It does not envy, it does not boast, it is not proud. It is not rude, it is not self-seeking, it is not easily angered, it keeps no record of wrongs" (vv. 4-5).

When *love* is used without a context or left undescribed, the word is weak and confusing. It may refer to an emotion, to romance or to having intercourse. Use and abuse has robbed the word *love* of its beauty and clarity. Consequently, even Jesus' central command to "Love him and your neighbor as yourself" is unclear.

If the world is going to hear God's good news, it needs to be repackaged. His eternal truth needs to be tuned to the times and communicated in concepts that connect with people in today's world.

Effective communication includes the element of surprise. Even when you have heard it before, it catches you off guard. It is like a catalyst in a chemical formula. A chain reaction of thoughts gets started.

I recently received a letter from Becky Pippert. An evangelist and a superb communicator, Becky stirred my mind with the statement: "We haven't come to the end of ourselves yet—so the church is still shocked by sin when she should be staggered by grace." *Sin* and *grace* are old words. They are weary and worn. But because sin and grace are still central in God's scheme for life, we must recraft them until they are poignant with meaning again.

Richard Pryor is someone else who sets off chain reactions. He is attributed with the quote: "Using drugs is the greatest feeling in the world unless you want to be a human being." I would like to paraphrase Mr. Pryor's good insight: "Living your life without God in this age is an alluring attraction unless you want to be a human being."

In a society that has so successfully blended culture and Christianity, it will be important for people to hear God's truth in a form that will provoke them to think—and then think again.

EMBRACING GOD'S DIVERSITY

I WAS SITTING IN MY FAMILY ROOM WHEN THE DOORBELL rang. As I walked down the hallway, I could see a well-dressed woman and an attractive young girl through the screen door. As I reached for the door handle, I saw the literature in their hands. "Jehovah's Witnesses," I thought.

The woman introduced herself and her daughter and then launched into her prepared speech. I interrupted in a quiet voice, "I am a serious Christian and not a potential convert." She had been well tutored. "Then we have a lot in common," was her quick reply.

I was not open to a lengthy discussion. The woman had her views. I had mine. Frankly, neither one of us was predisposed to really listen to each other. I tried to be gracious. She was courteous. The encounter at the door was brief. I had survived yet another interreligious dialog.

Dining in a Religious Smorgasbord

The plethora of religious options in our time is the consequence of living in a democratic society that places a high value on freedom and self-expression. The cultural commitment to "freedom of religion" has not only permitted but has encouraged the diversification of religion that exists today. It is no wonder that almost all in the society identify themselves as "religious somethings."

The globalization of the world's religions in North America is beginning to complicate matters even further. Consider the implications of setting up a prayer room in a public building in today's society. When there was a clear cultural consensus in North America that Christianity was right and the rest of the world simply needed to be Christianized, setting aside a room for prayer in a public institution was an easy matter. People in charge could simply decide to do it. They may not have received applause for their efforts, but the consensus was so strong, they would not be challenged.

The recent fiasco in the British Columbia Legislature's prayer room tells the modern story. The newspaper lead in reporting the chaos describes it well: "All hell broke loose in the prayer room yesterday."

There were duelling prayers. People spoke in tongues. Some people sang hymns. Others chanted mantras. There were shouting matches over who the true God is and whether God is male or female.

The prayer room was established by a group of fundamentalist evangelical Christians to pray for the members of the legislature. . . . But yesterday, it was invaded by a group of non-Christians, including Muslims, pagans and a Sufi—a member of an Islamic sect.

Security guards were eventually called to the weekly prayer meeting to restore order.[1]

At the end of the twentieth century in North America, our society is offering more alternatives on the religious menu than in former days. How can we respond to the increasing diversity? What attitudes should members of the different world religions have toward each other? How can differing denominations relate to each other and still maintain their commitments? What should be the disposition of Protestants toward Catholics and Catholics toward Protestants? As the New Age movement gains momentum, how should we respond to its claims regarding spirituality?

It is important that these matters be addressed. When non-Christians perceive that Christians do not have a healthy regard for each other, they think to themselves, "I don't want to live with those kind of attitudes." And further, when non-Christians sense that people who do follow Jesus have not worked out how to relate to those people who have rejected their Christ, they conclude that Christians are either insecure or elitist. Their response is "No thank you. I prefer my present views on life."

Jesus knew that unity was important for the future of the church. During his final week on earth, he prayed to his heavenly Father: "May they be brought to complete unity to let the world know that you sent me and have loved them even as you have loved me" (Jn 17:23). Richard Neuhaus reinforces Jesus' concern with his own strong words: "Perhaps Christians should, if they have the ecumenical nerve for it, first try to resolve the disputes among themselves before they attempt to articulate the implications of what they believe for the society at large."[2]

The mere existence of so many different churches, whether they are at peace with each other or not, can be an obstacle to evangelism. While speaking to a large group of high-school students, I was forcefully reminded that even the number of denominational choices can discourage some people from pursuing their interest in God.

I had been invited into a public school to share some of the research findings from a national survey of Canadian youth. After looking at some of the general results, I steered the group into the area of beliefs. Speaking from the data, I asked those senior teens why they claimed to believe in God but were not ready to go to church.

A number of the students simply saw no correlation between believing in God and attending church. From their point of view, affirming God's existence was quite a separate matter from participating in church life. Others spoke out specifically about there being too many churches.

"There's a church on every corner. Which one do you want us to attend?"

"One preacher says one thing; another claims something else. How should I know who's right?"

"Churches are always bickering with each other, anyway. Who needs the hassle? Count me out."

For that group of young people, the excessive number of churches—all claiming to be right and sometimes having difficulty getting along with each other—stood as obstacles between them and God. Can the obstacles be removed?

If history is any indicator, institutional unity is not a real alternative. Theological commitments and historical traditions are too entrenched to make agreement feasible. Institutions take a long time to develop and a much longer time to dismantle. In fact, there will probably be even more religious alternatives on the menu in the future than there have been in the past.

The wide range of belief choices and denominational options confronts us with religious pluralism. The issue inside the religious realm we need to resolve is exactly the same as we face in the culture itself: *How can we learn to respect each other's beliefs and live peaceably with our differences?*

New Testament Quarreling

The first-generation Christians were the original trendsetters. Even before Jesus could fully detail his game plan, his disciples were angling for positions of influence and power. Before the New Testament church was consolidated as a solid structure, it began to fragment. Even though one of Jesus' last prayers on earth was that disunity would not plague his people, there is clear evidence that internal division was part of early church life. Look at the details in 1 Corinthians 1—4 as an example.

There was infighting revolving around the distinct teachings of four separate leaders. The Scriptures speak with candor. "There are quarrels among you. What I mean is this: One of you says, 'I follow Paul'; another, 'I follow Apollos'; another, 'I follow Cephas'; still another, 'I follow Christ' " (1:11-12).

Peter Wagner has an insightful interpretation of the polarities inside the Corinthian church.[3] He contends that there were party factions around the various leaders.

First there was the Paul party, who were undoubtedly the original members of the church, the first converts won to Christ by Paul. You can almost hear them referring to "how the church used to be" and reminding people of "the good old days."

The second group were followers of Apollos, a converted Alexandrian Jew and Paul's replacement as the minister at Corinth, a man with a reputation as an eloquent and convincing preacher. Although it should be pointed out that there is no evidence that Apollos was articulating heretical teachings, Wagner proposes that Apollos's Platonist background may have led him to lean to the left in his interpretations of the faith and would thereby influence others to do the same.

The faithful followers of Peter (Cephas) were probably the legalists in the congregation. According to F. F. Bruce, the group of people who invoked Peter's authority probably represented a Judaizing tendency. If the Apollos loyalists were on the liberal side of the issues, the people attracted to Peter's emphases took the conservative position. They could be counted on to underscore the *don'ts* of the faith. They had deep convictions and strong feelings about the details of belief and behavior.

People who formed the fourth contingent inside the Corinthian church were the most pious. They were convinced that God's ways and their ways were synonymous. They had full-fledged memberships in Christ's party. They were the "corner on truth" people. Not to agree with them would place you under grave spiritual suspicion. They were right and not to agree with them meant you were wrong.

Beyond acknowledging that diversity is a given in life, what can we learn from our New Testament history? Obviously, Paul's letter did not resolve the debate. Almost two thousand years later, we still have church power-brokers who can only look backward and remember the good old days. Denominations that accommodate the liberals and conservatives and legalists are still with us. The modern church continues to harbor those who think they have God's final word on faith and life. What should our attitudes be toward the prevailing differences that will not go away? How can God's family at least begin to move toward each other?

God's Gift of Diversity

Before we go further, it is critical to acknowledge that the diversity is God's idea. Whether we look at God's creation in the plant, animal or human world, diversity is a basic fact of existence.

Scotch pines and blue spruces are a lot alike, but they are also dissimilar. A birch tree is easily identified when compared to a maple tree. A tiger lily is distinct from a daffodil. Carrots are not the same as cauliflower. A ruby-throated hummingbird, a bald eagle, a Jersey cow, an Arabian horse, a Boston terrier, a Persian cat and a grizzly bear are all members in good standing in the animal world, but they are far from being the same.

An assembly-line mentality was not in God's scheme for humans either. As a genetic engineer of human beings, God was especially creative. Our variety of skin colors, personality types, temperaments and range of learning styles all announce our diversity. The fact that even with billions of people in the world we can be individually identified by our fingerprints is astounding. Our different shapes and sizes, our unique laughs and distinct faces, some heads with hair and others without, our conglomeration of gifts and abilities, our likes and dislikes—all these combine to give us uniqueness. Only God could be inventive enough to make such an assortment possible.

Can there be any other conclusion? When God decreed that creation was good, he obviously decided that diversity was good too. God is for diversity. Our challenge is to learn to live with what he has put in place.

Diversity and Denominations

If denominations were not in God's original draft for organized religious life on earth, he has permitted the phenomenon to flourish. An obvious response is simply to acknowledge that both religious traditions and denominations exist and are not likely to pass away. The multifaceted approach to religious life in North America is as firmly entrenched as motherhood and government. And we should be grateful. Denominationalism is compatible with God's diversity in creation. The plethora of church choices serves the complexity of human nature and personal preferences.

In practice, the existence of church options accommodates the significant differences among God's big family. Sociologists have long observed that different churches serve distinctive constituencies. Denominational alternatives complement the sociological complexity of society. Just as some people enjoy Country and Western music, others prefer Brahms and Beethoven. Denominational alternatives not only respond to differing tastes in music, they expand the scope and size of the kingdom. They offer more contexts for more people to get to know God.

We need to realize that institutional structures are not sacred. They are constructed with human hands and are built out of both strengths and weaknesses. A grid that keeps organized structures in their right place calls for every church and tradition to see the components of their ecclesiastical life as a combination of *treasures, baggage* and *garbage.*[4]

The *treasures* are the denominational distinctives that give each structure its identity and strength. They are the riches that should be shared with the wider church. The treasures are those aspects of God's revelation that capture their adherents and stand out as being important to them. A glance at the list below will quickly reveal that any one denomination cannot feasibly emphasize more than a few of the strengths that are identified. However, when they are all corporately expressed, the extensive nature of God's truth and his ways are revealed to the bigger world. (The following lists are illustrative rather than comprehensive. They represent the biases and perceptions of the author. The reader is encouraged to reflect on his or her own church world and draft an adapted list.)

Treasures
   Worshipful liturgy
   Evangelistic fervor
   Social service
   Biblical preaching
   Integration of theory and practice
   High view of truth
   Personal Bible study
   Intellectual scholarship
   Emotional experiences
   Clear sense of mission
   Concern for the poor
   Global missions commitment
   Excellence in music
   Ecumenical concern
   Orientation to spiritual power
   Practice of prayer
   Holiness in lifestyle

Compassion
Relevance
Christian community
Use of spiritual gifts
Priesthood
Religious orders
Priesthood of all believers

The *baggage* is a part of the institutional ethos of church experience. It refers to the methodology of how things are done. The items listed relate more to external form than the essence of spiritual life. Yet, they are an important part of worship and church life.

Baggage
Raising one's hands
Crossing oneself
Kneeling benches
Altars
Confessional booths
Crucifixes
Prayer letters
Organ music
Hymns
Choruses
Prayer books
Orders of service
Small groups
Prayer meetings
Incense
Ethnic isolationism

The *garbage* is the long-term accumulation of stuff that could just as well be discarded. They are aberrations of God's truth. The garbage represents some of the good intentions of God's well-meaning people that have gone astray. They are the dark realities in organized religious life where the nudgings of God's Spirit have been set aside in favor of personal choice and human preference.

Garbage
Personal kingdom-building
Legalism
Relativism
Permissiveness
Begging for money
Dishonest prayer letters
Self-righteousness
Overemphasis of a single doctrine
Exclusivism
Universalism
Religious jargon

Churches are like automobiles. They have good features that operate well, and they have defects that cause them to break down. Both are used for a purpose that is outside of themselves. Cars take people places. They submit to the needs of the passengers. Churches are God's vehicles. They exist to arrange rendezvous between the Creator and those he created. Whenever religious leaders confuse the end with the means, the purpose of the church gets confused and life deteriorates.

Only Partly Right
At best, every church and religious system is a divine-human combination. The limits of humanness raise a sensitive issue for every denomination. Simply stated: *No denomination has all the truth.* In other words, every denomination, each religious tradition and every attempt to systemize theology are only partly right. The best that can be hoped for is an incomplete grasp of the whole.

The apostle Paul helps us at this point. Prompted by the inspiration of the Holy Spirit and realizing his limits this side of heaven, he wrote,

"We know in part and we prophesy in part. . . . Now we see but a poor reflection as in a mirror. . . . Now I know in part; then I shall know fully" (1 Cor 13:9, 12).

On this side of "knowing fully," we will be wise to be both true to our light and true to our darkness. That is, on the one hand, we will boldly claim what the Bible makes clear. On the other hand, we will not boldly claim what the Bible leaves unclear.

We can and must proclaim with conviction that Jesus died to redeem the whole world from sin and destruction. At the same time, when theologians extol their theories on the atonement, they should do so with appropriate caution. The Bible does not tell us exactly how Christ's death on the cross leads to our forgiveness. Holding to the light-and-darkness principle will prompt us to teach and assert the clear biblical teaching that "if you want to be forgiven, you must also live with a forgiving spirit." However, because of the ambiguity and darkness of the text, we must be less dogmatic when asserting our position on the millennium.

Our attitude needs to acknowledge our human subjectivity. A humble hermeneutic is the appropriate posture. We are not God. We cannot know all the truth. We are not able to take all the cosmic pieces of revelation and put them all together. Without entering into a discussion about the epistemology of knowing, my heart and head cry out, "A little humility, please." We need to accept the fact that no individual (including myself), or for that matter any single denomination or religious tradition, has the final word.

Modesty and Respect

Richard Neuhaus counsels that "whether we are dealing with alternative ways of being Christian or with other world religions, our approach must be marked by modesty and respect."[5] In other words, we need to surrender the "I'm right, and if you don't agree with me, you're wrong" attitude. The surrender does not need to lead to tentativeness or ambiguity. Rather, the invitation is to be faithful but humble. Arrogance is neither becoming nor Christlike.

Deep conviction shared with humility and modesty result in convincing communication. This posture delivers the message that truth can be known, but it also admits our human limitations. It acknowledges that God's truth is too complex and too comprehensive to be contained in the wisdom of an individual teacher, to be articulated in a systemized theology or even to be embraced by the expansive range of a historic religious tradition. In other words, God is too big and his wisdom too perplexing to be poured into a human container.

We would be better off to conceive the kingdom of God with its variety of religious traditions and denominations as an enormous stew. The church in the universal sense is an inordinate collection of meats and vegetables embroiled in a spicy sauce, all cooking together in a giant pot. In the final analysis, only God has the prerogative to decree who is not a part of the stew. Living with this attitude will dissipate the temptation to sit as judge and jury and rule on how other people worship and what they believe. Instead of channeling resources to critique and criticize others, energies can then be given to taking the mission of Christ into the world.

A Personal Posture

On a personal level, as we live in this stew and interact with Christians from other churches, we should accept the fact of diversity in this life and respect the genuineness of others who claim to be followers of Jesus.

Peter Mason, principal of Wycliffe College, an Anglican seminary at the University of Toronto, offers his insights:

> I think that Christians across denominational lines, and even across the major traditions of Catholic or liberal or charismatic streams, need to remember that the real enemy is not one another; the real enemy is the spirit of the age in which we live. That spirit declares that there is no God, no center of the universe. We have a major task to do in terms of proclaiming the truth and reality of

God to an age that does not know or believe or care, and it should unite us and put our differences into perspective.

That does not mean we repudiate the differences, for sometimes they are significant. But we must recognize that the world needs the good news of Christ, and if Catholics or Protestants or evangelicals are speaking it, then that should be the most significant fact prompting them to respect each other.[6]

Relating to Other Christians

One of the marks of God's creation is his expression of diversity. God has permitted the range of organized religious alternatives in this age to be many and varied. On the one hand, God uses the current array of churches as different means of inviting people to himself. On the other hand, the multitude of church choices is often confusing to those who may be open to God but have not encountered him personally. When individual Christians and even denominations invest their resources in critiquing and sometimes attacking each other, they not only squander their limited energy but they create evangelistic obstacles.

What then should be our disposition toward fellow believers who have different religious ideas and convictions from our own? We should relate to people from other religious traditions and denominations in the same manner as we respond to the people in our lives who are not Christians.

First, we should *accept* them. God has not assigned us the task of judging fellow believers. He has assumed the role of convicting and correcting his people. The church is God's to purify. We are better off to treat other Christians like we would like to be treated ourselves. Our role is to complement each other's faith and witness. Remembering that acceptance does not necessarily mean agreement or approval, we accept other Christians by saying, "I receive you. I welcome you. I extend my open spirit to you out of respect for what you claim to be."

Second, we should *appreciate* followers of Jesus who are from different churches and religious traditions than our own. We have more in common with Christians from other persuasions than we do with people of the society who have no concern for the things of God. What we share in common is far more important that what tends to separate us. We should confirm our agreements and celebrate what binds us together. Denominational loyalty is important, too, but it is not necessary for us to oppose others in order to affirm what is important to ourselves. A review of the list of denominational treasures will reveal that collectively the kingdom of God is a storehouse of riches. An awareness of the different shades of theology and the distinctive practices of other ways of thinking and worshiping should open Christians up to receive gifts from each other.

How else should we relate to fellow Christians? As long as we do not create further divisions, we have the freedom to debate with each other and to appropriately *influence* each other. Our influence should not be squandered by lobbying people from other churches to leave their places of worship in order to come to our own. Unless there are solid and serious reasons for doing so, that action fractures the church rather than building it up.

Rather, our influence should be spent encouraging reconciliation and affirming each other's faith in the risen Christ. We should build up rather than tear down. We should be looking for common ground and finding reasons to stand together.

As fellow Christians intentionally reaching across organizational distance, we will be able to stimulate each other to faith and good works. In a world that increasingly pressures everyone to disregard God, can we do better than use our influence to stimulate each other to pursue God and his ways? In a society that has relativized truth, can we do better than to use our influence to convey our confidence in the Scriptures as God's reliable and eternal revelation of what is true and right?

Whether we are at work, in a community affairs meeting, on the golf course, in a neighbor's kitchen or traveling on a bus, when it is apparent we are in the presence of another follower of Jesus, may we pray a prayer of thanksgiving for them and wish them a life of joyful obedience. If we live that way, Jesus will be pleased.

As I reflect back on one of my own experiences, I think Jesus was displeased. A few years ago I was in charge of coordinating an interdenominational student mission at the University of Alberta. Our deep desire was to make Jesus an issue on campus and call students to accept his claims on their lives.

In the early stages of the planning, we were able to plant the vision in all the religious clubs and denominational groups represented on the campus. That meant there were approximately fifteen organizations behind the venture. On the one side there were groups that people would call "liberal," and on the other side there were the "conservatives" and even a couple of groups many would label "fundamentalists." We attempted to create a context that encouraged each group to express their approach to evangelism in a bold way. We planned and prayed together. We strategized. We worked hard together.

Late one night my phone rang. A couple of the more conservative groups had been in a long meeting. They were displeased. They felt they could no longer associate with the mission venture. They had just heard that in the context of the mission some of the more liberal groups were planning to show a film that they could not endorse. God's Spirit was directing them to disassociate themselves with the whole affair, they said..

The university student newspaper gave priority to reporting the incident. My guess is that non-Christians read the account and responded with a "so what else is new" nod. "There go those Christians fighting with each other again."

When the Christian family puts each other down, they discourage those who are not God's people from becoming God's people. On the other hand, when Christian unity prevails, obstacles to believing in Jesus are removed.

The Symphony

Wouldn't the world take the claims of Christianity more seriously if the universal Christian church were more like Jesus directing a massive symphony orchestra?

Can you picture Jesus standing on the conductor's rostrum, baton in hand, the whole orchestra waiting for his commands? The violin section would be made up of players from the mainline denominations. The Catholics would fill the section assigned for the cellos and bass violins. Evangelical types would take their places in the brass section with their saxophones in hand. The trumpets would be tended by the fundamentalists. The drums and cymbals would be in the hands of the independent ethnic churches.

The music on the program would range from standard classics to the most modern scores. Some of the sounds would be loud and boisterous. Other moments would be quiet and mellow. Throughout the program, each section would alternatively have the spotlight focused just on them. There would be no guest artist.

And the music, the music would capture you. It would take you beyond yourself into the presence of God himself.

If Jesus were on earth again, I wonder if we would let him call his church together so we could play his Father's music? Would we let him be the conductor? Jesus' prayer to his heavenly Father remains as a noble aspiration for us to pursue: "May they be brought to complete unity to let the world know that you sent me" (Jn 17:23).

Chapter Seven

PERSONALIZING OUR WITNESS

I N TODAY'S WORLD, MOTHER TERESA IS THE MODEL OF a modern Christian. This sensitive but strong-willed woman of Calcutta personifies Christlikeness. God and the media have lifted her up before the eyes of the world—and the world perceives that she is both godly and good. Indeed, Mother Teresa is "something beautiful for God."[1]

On numerous occasions I have invited audiences, Christian and otherwise, to make word-association responses to the images they carry of Mother Teresa. Inevitably, the mention of her name will elicit replies of "caring, sacrifice, self-giving, life, joy, compassion" and also "Christian." On no occasion has anyone said "Roman Catholic" or even "a nun." Mother Teresa has transcended her organizational identity.

The perceptions around Mother Teresa are partly explained by the trends of the time. We are a culture that believes more in people than in organizations.

The Age of Person-Power

Chrysler strategically and effectively fronts its chief executive officer, Lee Iacocca, as the "modern messiah" of business. One series of television advertisements featured Mr. Iacocca in a posh office setting just talking about his company's virtues. A shiny new car was not even pictured. In essence, the message was, "Trust me. Believe in me." When some of Chrysler's dealers were caught selling used cars as new models, the "modern messiah" was called in for the rescue. Full-page newspaper ads were run across the country featuring Lee's picture and personal apology along with his reassurances that anyone who was mistreated would be generously compensated.

The entertainment scene plays the same tune. Bill Cosby consistently makes the top-ten list of entertainment earnings each year. A truly funny man, he parades into more living rooms than any of his competitors. The television series bearing his name is a vehicle for him to both share his humor and convey his philosophy. His two recent books have each sold millions of copies. Cosby is not only a modern hero, he is a powerful person in the culture. And one reason that is true is because we live in a culture hungry for human heroes.

In the political arena, Mikhail Gorbachev not only made it onto the cover of *Time* magazine, but he is a leader whose time has come. He exudes self-confidence. Utilizing the appeal of his personal charisma, walking among the common people and pitching his platform on television, Gorbachev is seizing his moment in history. He is pressing his policies of *glasnost* (openness) and *perestroika* (economic reform) with the might of his personality and the power of his position. He personifies a confident spirit, and people are ready to believe in him.

A Moscow-based Western diplomat declared, "For the first time here, there is a feeling that almost anything could be possible."

A person from the religious realm who deserves respect and confidence and who as a result stands tall in the culture is Billy Graham. While some of his evangelist-colleagues have publicly disgraced themselves and God's good name, Dr. Graham continues to preserve his integrity and conduct himself with dignity. Even with the spirit of secularism in control of the culture, his credibility is acknowledged and affirmed. On August 6, 1988, the Saturday edition of Canada's national newspaper, *The Globe and Mail*, featured a front-page picture and positive story on Billy Graham and his long-term commitment to evangelism.

Today's world is oriented to people. Person power is potent. Ideology is being pushed into the background by personal charisma. In the workplace, in politics, in business and in the realm of religion, the populace is looking for people they can trust. They are ready to place their confidence in people who deserve to be believed in.

In this person-oriented age, friendship is highly valued. In the case of teen-agers and young adults in their twenties, friendship is both their number-one value and their highest perceived source of enjoyment.[2] At least eight out of ten older adults claim that friendship is very important to them.[3]

There is consequently no surprise in the claim that friendship is a vehicle for influence. Life simply works that way. Being influenced by what we value is as automatic as feeling tired after a long day's work. When you ask an audience to identify who has been most influential in their decisions to become Christians and follow Christ, there are two predominant responses: family and friends. Relationships are at the center of modern life. Relationships between serious followers of Jesus and those who believe otherwise are both gifts to be enjoyed and opportunities for building up God's church.

The possibilities for evangelism are astonishing. In practical terms, the temperament of the times invites interpersonal interaction. The predominance of the Christian religious heritage in North America has left people open to God. They are ready for appropriate conversations with significant people in their lives about what is important to them and what they believe. Their dormant inclination toward the Christian faith can be awakened. When committed Christians earn the trust and inspire the confidence of those who do not care very much about God in this culture, they can have the privilege of influencing those people toward a life-changing relationship with Christ.

The Boomerang Effect

One reason for the increasing desire for personal relationships is the backlash from technological developments. In his book *Megatrends*, John Naisbitt develops a chapter around the theme of "High-Tech/High-Touch." His premise is solid. He simply states, "The more high technology around us, the more the need for human touch."[4]

Computers are a major part of the technological world that is invading almost every realm of life. It will be some time before we will be able to understand the total effect of the new "computer culture" on us. Although we are unable to be completely definitive, there is a sense that "technology is fast outstripping the pace of political and social adjustment."[5] We do know, however, that our hands-on experience with technological gadgets and electronic computer wizardry does instill a craving in us for the human touch. These experiences with the tools of our time can also trigger negative emotional reactions.

Consider the impact of telephone answering machines. How do you feel when you dial the number of a friend and you get a voice on tape? Even if the message is clever and there is soothing music playing in the background, one tends to feel cheated. And what about call-waiting? When I hear that beep signaling another incoming call, I feel devalued, no matter how courteously my friend asks, "Can I put you on hold for a moment?" And how do you handle one of those automatic computer-dialed calls trying to sell you something when your phone rings during the supper hour? Technology can leave a bad aftertaste.

The mass availability of banking machines is having both positive and negative consequences on human behavior. Certainly the machines are accessible and efficient. Being able to make transactions at any time of the day or night can virtually eliminate the need to stand in a long line. However, what happens when it is necessary to stand in a long line to wait for the services of a human teller? When one is not used to waiting it is a challenge to treat the person across the counter with a patient spirit.

On the other hand, the whole experience is altered when you bank at a small branch where you know the tellers by name and they also know you. Even when the wait is longer than you wish, life is less stressful when you go to the counter saying, "Good afternoon, Brenda, what is your day like?" Whenever life is personalized, it elevates the human experience. Technology is feeding the desire in us to get personal.

Disillusionment with institutions is also pulling us toward each other. Regrettably, the affirmation of life at the interpersonal level is coming at the expense of confidence levels that used to be placed in institutions and organizations.

The perpetuation of the war in Vietnam, Watergate, hostages in Iran, insider trading on Wall Street, scandals among religious leaders, illegal sleaze by political and military leaders and immorality among presidential contenders—all these have taught us not to put our hopes in institutions. Organizations are now primarily viewed as means for achieving personal ends.

The coldness of technological living and our growing disbelief in bigness and bureaucracy have left us clinging to ourselves and each other. If today's committed followers of Jesus will faithfully engage the people God brings within the range of their personal influence with a credible understanding of the gospel, the current state of affairs will lead to real progress for the kingdom.

Free to Be Ourselves

If Jesus were to pay a visit to North America, he would not have to adapt his style of engaging people. Despite two thousand years and a few thousand miles, his manner and method of relating the gospel is exactly what is effective today.

Conference speaker and businessman Gene Thomas delights in pointing out to audiences that "Jesus allowed people around him to be their natural rotten selves." He goes on to cite how the disciples felt free to squabble within the range of Jesus' hearing about who would be awarded the positions of president and minister of finance when the new kingdom was set up (Lk 9:46).

There was something about Jesus' accepting attitude that gave people in his presence permission slips to be what they really were. His demeanor allowed prostitutes to be in the same room with him without being embarrassed. People with reputations as sinners were relaxed around him. Jesus was accused of being a "drunkard, a friend of tax collectors and sinners" (Mt 11:19). Undoubtedly the charge was not because Jesus drank too much, but because people around him were doing so. Sinners did not feel alienated around Jesus. He made them feel comfortable.

Jesus extended uncensored acceptance toward the people who entered his life. There is nothing in the New Testament record to indicate that Jesus ever conveyed an attitude toward people that called them to conform to his preferences before they received a serious hearing. This did not mean Jesus affirmed the status quo in their lives. That is not the same thing as acceptance. What he perceived often distressed him, but he was always able to see potential in the people he encountered.

Yet Jesus related to people as they were before projecting what they could be. And people sensed his openness toward them and felt free about moving closer to him.

Thomas's Freedom

The disciple Thomas was just one example of many who felt safe enough to be transparent in Jesus' presence.

When Jesus was nearing the end of his earthly ministry, he was offering reassurance to his disciples: "Do not let your hearts be troubled. . . . In my Father's house are many rooms. . . . I am going there to prepare a place for you. . . . You know the way to the place where I am going" (Jn 14:1-4).

Instead of nodding his head as if he understood, without any pretense and with vulnerable candor, Thomas replied, "Lord, we don't know where you are going, so how can we know the way?" (v. 5).

After Jesus' crucifixion and resurrection, the stakes were a lot higher for Thomas, but he behaved in the same honest manner. Jesus had already made a post-resurrection appearance to the disciples, but Thomas was not present at the time. The others tried to convince Thomas that Jesus was alive, but his skepticism overruled his faith. The disciple, renowned for his struggle to believe, decreed: "Unless I see the nail marks in his hands and put my finger where the nails were, and put my hand into his side, I will not believe it" (Jn 20:25).

When Jesus appeared before his disciples a second time, Thomas was there too. Jesus had every reason to either reject, ignore or even condemn Thomas's skepticism. For Thomas had all kinds of history and experiences with Jesus that should have put his doubts to rest.

After he came into the room where his disciples were gathered, Jesus greeted his men with, "Peace be with you!" Then he turned toward Thomas and said, "Put your finger here; see my hands. Reach out your hand and put it into my side. Stop doubting and believe" (Jn 20:26-27). Thomas declared, "My Lord and my God!" (v. 28).

The encounter between Jesus and Thomas did not end with Thomas's declaration of belief. Jesus seized the situation to stretch Thomas's perceptions about faith. As the other disciples listened, Jesus began to teach: "Because you have seen me, you have believed; blessed are those who have not seen and yet have believed" (Jn 20:29).

In this situation with Thomas, Jesus simply followed his normal approach to people. He always personalized his encounters with people. His interaction with individuals was not preprogrammed. He was always situation- and person-specific. No two conversations were ever the same. Jesus inherently valued people. Whether it was a disciple or a chance encounter, Jesus took their concerns and perceptions seriously. Consequently, when people were with Jesus, they had a sense that they mattered.

While being flexible and person-oriented, Jesus was never gullible nor naive. "His words, always tailored to the individual's needs, never failed to puncture an inquirer's self-righteousness, unveil wrong motives, or warn of false faith or shallow commitment."[6] Consequently, what Jesus demonstrated with Thomas and with other people who intersected his life stands as a pattern for us today.

Loving and Enjoying People

A few weeks ago I met Mike, a big man in his late thirties. He is the owner and operator of a small printing plant. Early in our discussion I discovered Mike likes to employ young people to work in his shop. He started talking about some of his people.

Pam is Mike's eighteen-year-old receptionist. He described her as "bright and well-intentioned, but still eighteen." After Pam had been working for about nine months, she bounded into Mike's office to announce that she had a wonderful opportunity to go to England for three weeks. Then she asked for the time off. Mike replied, "Well, you know I'm going to let you go, but would you find someone to cover for you while you're gone?" Mike smiled as he talked about giving Pam a hundred-pound note at the office going-away party.

Mike was in a musing mood by this time, and he began talking about Larry. "He's around twenty-five years old and is into some strange religion. We don't know much about it, but he does a good job and we respect him. Larry got into some financial trouble last year, and we were able to help him out of his problem. Part of my philosophy is to give our people guidelines and then let them go at it. I believe everyone should have the right to succeed or fail."

I was curious. I asked him, "How did you come to all these beliefs? Who helped shape your management style?"

He must have had a hunch that I was a religious type because he immediately pointed out, "I was never in a church until the day I got married. I just grew up that way. My belief structure is just a part of my life. It's just the way I am."

I probed deeper. "Who has been most influential in your life?"

Mike's response was immediate. "That's easy. My mother and my father. My mother was a lover, and my father was a worker. They taught me great things." Mike moved on to start talking about his own children and how he hoped to influence them. "I think loving your kid is taking them to the hockey rink and playing with them—not just dropping them off."

Mike isn't a Christian, but spending time with him makes you wish you could emulate some of his fine qualities. He is so personable, so alive. He loves people and enjoys them. A thoughtful and generous spirit flows out of him. He believes in the people who work for him. He sees potential in his employees and goes beyond just signing their paychecks. He cares for his people and risks for them. In many ways, Mike is like Jesus. He would be a magnificent Christian.

By contrast, committed Christians who do not genuinely love and care for people will be handicapped when it comes to witnessing for Christ in the world. Words that convey the right information but lack a sense of personal concern will have limited impact in this age. People who claim to love God but display little love for the people in their lives will have a very limited sphere of redemptive influence. They are too unlike Jesus to represent him effectively.

Looking beneath the Secular Veneer

Non-Christians like Mike can be a threat to some followers of Jesus. Mike's natural temperament is pleasant and appealing. His outgoing personality and accepting attitude invite people to relax around him. His social I.Q. is high.

We need to remember, however, that natural gifts and the extraordinary abilities possessed by non-Christians should not be confused with human completeness. No one on the face of this earth "has it all together." Regardless of the level of native ability and socialized development, everyone has a dark side, a nature that is inclined toward sin and selfishness. Looking beneath the secular veneer that covers people will reveal the true inner life of those who do not know God.

A deeper look inside those who are not yet Christians will frequently reveal both a sensitivity to sin and the reality of incompleteness. People do not go around making announcements about their inside stories. If they are insecure, they are more likely to cover up their inadequacies than expose them. If they are feeling guilty, the inclination is to quiet their guilt rather than reveal it. The same pattern is true with acknowledging sin and incompleteness. Most people shy away from exposing their vulnerability. But based on our understanding of human nature and our own behavioral patterns, we can begin to make some assumptions about others and look for indicators of what is really hidden inside.

For instance, even though adultery is common, and the majority of adults who are not married are sexually active, there is a lingering consensus that promiscuity is bad. The Christian memory in North American society is not dead. Looking for the cracks in the armor of those who appear to be healthy and self-sufficient will often reveal tender consciences, doubts, inner anxiety and the longing for something more in this life.

Urban ministry specialist Gary Nelson knows how to look beneath the secular veneer. He talks about his experience of living in a big-city apartment block. After months of common courtesies and social initiatives, he overcame the reputation of being a minister on the prowl for converts and established himself as a normal person who

lived in the building. Gary knew the people on his floor were practicing different sexual lifestyles than he condoned. Still, he entertained his neighbors and was a guest in their homes too. They got
beyond surface conversation and really liked each other. His experience prodded him to look deep and insightfully ask, "Why do we
religious types so often view a sexual encounter as lust rather than
loneliness?"

Assessing the behavior of people on external appearances alone is
like evaluating the structural support of a floor by looking at the
carpet. It is an incomplete view. And if there is a desire to really
understand people and be a presence for God in their lives, it is
inadequate.

Being Person-Specific

In this age, where relationships rule and person power is potent,
communication of the gospel that is impersonal is both inadequate
and ineffective. That was the message of the young woman who
looked across the table at me and challenged, "Don't just quote the
Bible at me. Nothing is more horrible than having quotations thrown
at you."

Impersonal witnessing is like getting a birthday card from your
insurance agent. Your reaction is to trash it. But what's involved in
being personal in one's style of witness? How does one explain the
gospel to non-Christians so that it is not automatically discarded?

Listen and discover. Witnessing that is personal is receiver-centered
rather than sender-oriented. Though we want to convey God's ways,
we must first listen and discover where others are in their spiritual
journey. The intent is to ascertain what a good starting place would
be for the dialog to begin. If someone is wondering whether or not
God exists, attempting to explain the significance of Christ's death is
not fruitful. If a person has no sense of spiritual need, there is no
point in talking about repentance. Discovering people's history,
understanding something of their family background and determin-

ing their previous exposure to the claims of the gospel are all prerequisites to appropriate personal witnessing.

Adapt and apply. When the lawyer came to Jesus asking about inheriting eternal life, eventually Jesus told him the parable of the Good Samaritan and instructed him to "go and do likewise" (Lk 10:25-37). When Thomas stood before Jesus filled with doubt and anxiety, Jesus extended his hands in reassurance and invited his doubting disciple to physically touch him (Jn 20:24-29). In the case of Zacchaeus, Jesus went to his house for an evening of "tax talk" which led to forthright confession and restitution (Lk 19:1-10). Jesus was not an advocate of "xerox evangelism."[7] Without compromising the truth of the message, he adapted his communication so that it applied to the circumstances of the person in his presence. He personalized the message so that it connected with the concerns of the inquirer. Jesus' example stands as the standard for those who desire to personalize their witness in today's world.

Share and reveal. The point of personal evangelism is to be personal. Use your interpersonal influence for Christ's sake. When you are in a small group or just with another person, the natural thing to do is to share your own story. An honest account of your own story revealing how God became a central part of your life is often persuasive.

Be strong and weak. Whether you are sharing your personal testimony or communicating some other aspect of the gospel, "be true to your light and be true to your darkness." Tell your own story with excitement but do not make it all bright and beautiful. Tell all the truth of the gospel you know, but do not overpromise on God's behalf.

During an evangelism training session with some business people, a middle-aged man interrupted with a confession and a question. He explained that he had been a Christian for many years and that he wanted to let the people in his world know he was committed to his faith. Then he went on to say, "My difficulty is that I'm not sure I'm much different from my colleagues and my customers. They are concerned about money. I'm concerned about money. They have personal problems. I have personal problems. We look pretty similar. Do I keep silent about my struggles? What do I tell them?"

The answer is clear. God's people are people of truth. We tell both sides of the truth. We articulate our deep convictions that God created the world, that Christ died to rescue us from our sin and separation from him, and that we are learning to live as his followers. We also own where we are in our growth or lack of growth in Christ. We confess that our theory exceeds our practice, and we assert our commitment to persevere and mature in Christ.

Converse and listen. Witnessing that has the personal touch will not result in one individual "talking at" another individual. Instead, the person communicating God's truth will come alongside and engage the other person in purposeful and progressive discussion. Following a morning consulting session with a group of educators, I found myself over lunch interacting with a vice principal in a discussion about his spiritual journey. He was candid: "I stopped going to church when I was fourteen years old because I realized the people in the church were always preaching at me rather than standing with me."

All I could do was express my regret that he had a bad experience and invite him to take an adult look at the faith. His response was candid: "The big problem with religion from my adult point of view is that it is a deductive system. In other words, you have to accept what is already decided for you."

I countered: "Yes, a lot of life has been predetermined, but the journey of faith is also highly inductive. What God really wants is for us to discover what he has done and make personal decisions about his ways."

We talked and listened to each other for a long time.

People who posture a sense of superiority push others away from themselves and their ideas. People who project concern without any sense of condescension are more likely to attract others to themselves and create intrigue about what they think about life. Personal witnessing that tends to "put down" people is simply ineffective.

Witnessing that is characterized by confrontation in this age will also fail. Although there is a time to be persuasive and call for a definitive decision to accept Christ, the tenor of fruitful interpersonal evangelism is not confrontational. Rather, the tone of the witness is empathetic and compassionate.

And remember, witnessing that is person-specific is not only fruitful, it is enjoyable.

Deserving Respect

After working on the biography of Picasso for six years and coming to the conclusion that the artist's personal life was filled with flaws that harmed others around him, author Arianna Huffington rightly concluded: "We've reached a turning point. The character of an individual is now more judged than his works."[8]

The breach of public trust in recent years by politicians, business tycoons, brokers on Wall Street, religious leaders and athletes has left people feeling victimized. As a result, the matter of personal integrity is rightfully on the social agenda. There is a growing concern that people in high places have the character credentials to go along with their positions. The concern is not just restricted to people and situations that get reported in the media. The same phenomena filters down to interpersonal relationships. Individuals who are not perceived to be trustworthy have little influence on others around them.

In order for personal evangelism to have validity, particularly in these times, there must be coherence between the message and the messenger. The character of the person articulating the claims of the gospel needs to coincide with the theory being communicated. Unless the person speaking deserves respect, the message will be viewed with suspicion.

Although fraudulent people can still speak the truth, the power of the message is dependent on the integrity of the messenger. Fraudulence in the character of the communicator of God's truth fosters cynicism. The absence of integrity in God's people does not inspire faith.

At the same time we realize that if it is necessary to be flawless before one is qualified to speak God's good news, then the gospel will be sealed in silence forever. Being perfect is not a prerequisite for fruitful witnessing. Being grateful for what God has done and demonstrating a commitment to grow in Christ and pursue his ways will elicit respect. The Scriptures give good counsel to those who are feeling inadequate: "My grace is sufficient. . . . My power is made perfect in weakness" (2 Cor 12:9).

Using Your Relational Leverage

A frequent criticism leveled at any emphasis that encourages personal evangelism is that it reduces relationships to projects. The accusation can be valid. If people seek out friendships for the express purpose of witnessing to a prospective convert, the person becomes a task. Reducing relationships to evangelistic ventures is demeaning and an insult to the inherent value of people.

Because people stand at the pinnacle of God's creation, every relationship is a gift to be treasured. Because God has placed such a high value on human life, when people are treated as objects, their worth is slurred.

The concern about demeaning people or taking advantage of them can also be taken too far. Sometimes committed Christians are overly sensitive about using their relational leverage as an entry point for witnessing. Attempting to influence another person or sway someone's opinion is as normal in a day's events as getting out of bed in the morning. Parents begin setting standards for their children before they learn to walk. Friends presume upon each other's time and lead each other into shared interests. Preachers use their pulpits and counseling sessions to urge people to alter their behavior. Schoolteachers set agendas for their students every day of the school year. Politicians parade their best selves in an appeal for votes. Advertisers chant their claims in a never-ending quest to sell their products and separate people from their money. Persuasion of one sort or another is an everyday ingredient of life. Yet many of God's people resist inviting their friends to consider Christ and his promise of abundant life.

At the end of the school term, a group of InterVarsity staff workers were asked to describe the circumstances in which they saw university students becoming Christians. The list of people who had placed their faith in Christ that particular term was encouraging. There were new believers who were roommates of Christian students; some had come with their friends to a Bible study; international students had brought others from their own country to the group; and one Christian student had made a connection while demonstrating against apartheid. Even though the circumstances were unique in each instance, there was one common thread: everyone who had reached out to receive Christ did so because they had first been in a significant relationship with a student who already knew Christ.

Conviction and Compassion

This chapter began by focusing on Mother Teresa. Recently the Nobel-Prize-winning follower of Jesus addressed 15,000 demonstrators at an anti-abortion, pro-life rally. In a bold voice, Mother Teresa called abortion "a terrible evil." "Give the children to me instead" was her plea.[9]

One of the reasons God has allowed this tattered and worn older woman to be lifted up in his name is that Mother Teresa's faith combines the virtues of conviction ("Abortion is a terrible evil") and compassion ("Give the children to me").

Mother Teresa's behavior flows out of her unbending and tough-minded spiritual convictions. The theory of her deep-rooted faith is lived out in her principled behavior. She is ready to denounce what she believes is wrong. But her strong words are injected with compassion and a personal readiness to sacrifice.

Religion without conviction is shallow and worldly. Religion without compassion is rigid and inhumane. Conviction without compassion is harsh. Compassion without conviction is spineless. In God's created order, the virtues of compassion and conviction are meant to link arms and stand together.

People who wear the badge of both conviction and compassion in this age are compelling to others. Their principles give them strength. Their empathy graces them with sensitivity. When followers of Jesus who incarnate these two powers live among people who have little regard for God, the gospel is heard and seen as good news.

Chapter Eight

USING
OUR
MINDS

I*DEAS THAT FAIL TO TRANSLATE FROM THEORY INTO* practice eventually get discarded. When the idea of making money by investing in the stock market results in financial losses instead of gains, investing in the market eventually ceases.

The Christian claim that "God answers prayer" is subject to the same consequences. Unless there is some evidence that God does respond to the prayers of his people, even faithful people stop praying. Whether the strategies and claims of life apply to economics or religion, if ideas are not proved true by experience, the ideas and the practice of the ideas are abandoned.

The same correlation exists between our heads and our hearts. To be more specific, theories that receive our mental assent need to be endorsed by the experiences of our hearts before they are fully believed. There is a big difference between intellectually claiming "I believe God exists" and "knowing" God exists because of experiencing him. Ideas that ring true in our thinking need to be confirmed at the feeling level of our experience.

God created us to both think and feel. We should not be surprised that God has designed what we call Christianity to encounter the realms of both our hearts and our heads—the affective and cognitive domains of our humanity.

The Christian faith addresses both the affective and the cognitive sides of life. On the one hand, the Christian faith touches our hearts. It affects our inner life. When we encounter Christ, we receive his spiritual presence into our everyday world.

The Christian faith also connects with reality as we perceive it in our heads. Christianity is ideological. It comprises many ideas. It is truth to nurture and challenge our inquisitive minds. When Christianity is conceived as both a relationship and as a world view, the theory of our faith can be lived as a holistic experience.

Christianity as Relationship

As image-bearers of the God who created us, we long for relationships, for experiences that touch our hearts. Lawrence Crabb, in his book *Understanding People,* proposes that our need to be in significant relationships is due to the fact that God exists as a trinity: three persons, one God. "There is relationship within the very nature of God. God is a personal being who exists eternally in a relationship among persons: He is His own community." God designed his human creation "with a unique ability to respond to His love by choosing to enter into relationship with both Him and other similar beings. God created man for relationship with Himself and others. Man is fundamentally a relational creature."[1] In other words, God's attitude is: "I would like you to know me, and I would like to know you."

Jesus says to us, "Here I am! I stand at the door and knock. If anyone hears my voice and opens the door, I will come in and eat with him, and he with me" (Rev 3:20).

There is no hint that Jesus is interested in a forced entry into people's lives. Using a sledgehammer to break doors down is not his way. Picking the locks on doors so he can sneak in unnoticed is inconsistent with his character. Rather, Jesus' eternal knocking is the expression of his desire to be in relationship, to come alongside and "eat together." To open the door and let Jesus enter is comparable to spending a long evening with friends over a fine meal.

Having a special meal with friends is an invitation to intimacy. A quiet, unhurried evening with candlelight invites significant conversation. Eating and drinking, talking casually or confidentially, listening intently and laughing spontaneously all feed into deepening care for those around the table. Eating together is one of the most relational things we do.

Responding to Jesus is a relational encounter. It invades the realm of our hearts. Those who personally encounter Jesus as Savior know in the depths of their being that he is not just a theoretical idea—he is real. The theory of the cross translates into a high-touch personal experience.

Christianity as a World View

Because the Christian faith is constructed out of the components of God's truth, life in Christ also engages the mind. Being a Christian involves the realm of our heads.

Faith stands on ideas that help make sense out of the complexity of modern life and bring meaning into our personal experiences. Although the Christian faith is much more than a philosophical system, it does provide a coherent and integrated view of the whole of life. The acts of God in history, the life and teachings of Jesus and the mass of biblical content provide the construction material out of which an intellectual pattern for thinking and living can be built.

Consequently, thoughtful followers of Jesus are able to commit to specific values, embrace codes of ethics, carve out positions on personal and public morals, establish convictions about individual lifestyles and, in general, construct harmonious world views that are distinctly Christian.

Presenting Christianity's distinctive philosophy of life can be an effective way of attracting people to the faith. For instance, during the student election campaign at one university, the InterVarsity Christian Fellowship group sponsored an evening on the theme of "leadership." The leaders of the group invited the student presidential candidates to come and each make ten-minute presentations to their prospective voters. They also invited me to speak on the subject of "A Christian View of Leadership." For me, the most interesting aspect of the evening happened after most of the audience had left. One of the presidential candidates inadvertently exposed his view of Christianity when he said: "You know, what you said about leadership made sense, whether you are a Christian or not."

On another occasion, I addressed a group of professionals who had a special vocational interest in young people. After the session, one of the social workers present asked for a private discussion. We went for a walk. It turned out that he had recently separated from his wife and he was looking for help. I suggested that if he wanted to follow up on our time together that he call my office.

A week later, my secretary, Marilyn, handed me a telephone message from the same social worker. Then she said, "Let me tell you about my conversation with him. We were sorting out the details of how you had met and then he said, 'I'm not into Don's religion, but his philosophy of life is marvelous.' "

Many non-Christians, and too many Christians, have a narrow view of the scope of Christianity. They do not see the Christian faith speaking definitively to subjects like leadership. In their understanding, religion applies more to personal piety and private morality than to the wider issues of life. Consequently, those who do not see the broader parameters of the faith tend to separate religion from something as central as one's philosophy of life. This distortion and lack of comprehension about the true nature of the faith is a great tragedy.

A similar distortion occurs when Christians conceive of the gospel primarily as a religious-philosophical system. In his book *After Fundamentalism,* Bernard Ramm points out that Karl Barth was perpetually worried that "faith will be converted into knowledge. . . . Systems do not save; only the gospel saves. When the appeal of Christianity is its appeal as a great intellectual system then faith has been converted into knowledge."[2] Overintellectualizing the faith can rob the gospel of its transforming power. Underintellectualizing the faith can limit the scope of the gospel to personal salvation and morality.

Christians who conceive Christianity in both relational and ideological terms have the potential of encountering their Creator as whole persons. They also will have expanded opportunities to communicate the gospel in more meaningful terms to secularized people in the modern world.

Going Deep in the Faith
In Colossians Paul talks of the importance of thinking deeply about our faith and the influences of the world on it:

> So then, just as you received Christ Jesus as Lord, continue to live in him, rooted and built up in him, strengthened in the faith as you were taught, and overflowing with thankfulness. See to it that no one takes you captive through hollow and deceptive philosophy, which depends on human tradition and the basic principles of this world rather than on Christ. (2:6-8)

Paul immediately follows his affirmation of the Colossae Christians' faith ("you received Christ") with a sequence of instructions emphasizing the need to "continue to live in him."

The distinction between "beginning" and then "continuing" in the relationship with Christ is critical. Too often our modern evangelistic techniques overemphasize the decision to believe in Jesus and "become a Christian." When that happens, too little attention is given to consolidating the decision and moving on to "being a Christian." This preoccupation ends up producing many 100-meter-sprint Christians but too few long-distance marathoners. It is the "difference between paint, which is merely laid on the surface, and a dye or stain which soaks right through."[3]

Paul's injunction to his readers is to get "rooted" in Christ, be "built up in him," be "strengthened in the faith as you were taught" and be "thankful" (v. 7). In other words, go deep in the faith and do so "in a continuous process."[4] The urging is to persevere and to go on to maturity in Christ.

Becoming a Christian and *being* a Christian are like sunshine and warmth—they are inseparable. One does not exist without the other. Consequently, Paul links "receiving Christ" with being "built up in him." He is anxious to discourage spiritual anorexia. He knows that believers who remain as "mere infants in Christ" are susceptible to premature spiritual death (1 Cor 3:1).

Next Paul calls Christians to be on their guard while they are on their journey of faith. The game plan of complementing a strong offense with a solid defense is important in more areas of life than the sports arena. Paul sees the combination as an effective strategy for being a Christian in the world. His offensive tactics are to "receive Christ" and "be built up in him." His approach on defense is to live for Christ in the world but to do so while "no one takes you captive through hollow and deceptive philosophy" (Col 2:8). Paul warns us to look for the lies.

Frederick Buechner talks of being struck by the lies in our world one day while riding on a train. He describes a cigarette ad he saw across the aisle from where he was sitting. "There was a pretty girl in it and a good-looking boy, and they were sitting together somewhere—by a mountain stream, maybe, or a lake, with a blue sky overhead, green trees. It was a crisp, sunlit scene full of beauty, of youth, full of *life* more than anything else. . . . And then down in the lower left-hand corner of the picture, in letters large enough to read from where I was sitting, was the Surgeon General's familiar warning."

Buechner reflected that he had seen such ads thousands of times, but on this occasion the pretty picture triggered a fatal message: "Buy this; it will kill you." "Choose out of all that is loveliest and greenest and most innocent in the world that which can make you sick before your time and bring your world to an end. Live so you will die."[5]

Perhaps even more dangerous than cigarettes, however, are the many ways our culture offers other, more subtle invitations to lives that are hazardous to our health: the chant of the culture that God is unnecessary; the appeal to self-fulfillment above all else; the temptations to willfully choose disobedience; the lure to be autonomous; the denial of manipulative motives; the drive to make more money; the compulsion to consolidate power; the appetite for illicit sex; the enticements for more personal pleasure; the urging to disregard the needs of others. All these inclinations point the way to death instead of life.

In many ways, life is the competition of ideas to gain the allegiance of more adherents. It is no wonder God spoke through Paul to warn his people to watch out, to be careful not be to seduced by the ways of the world. Unless we resist, we will be conned into believing what counters the teachings of Christ.

The ways of the world are often inviting. Satan is shrewd. He is the master of the masquerade (2 Cor 11:14). And he is a patient opportunist. He can be counted on to return again and again—at a more "opportune time" (Lk 4:13). Without the "full armor of God" and without the presence of the indwelling Holy Spirit, the people of God are vulnerable to the world's persuasions and Satan's temptations (Eph 6:13).

God is fully aware of the reality of the spiritual warfare facing modern Christians. Our great hope to persevere and overcome is that

God has committed himself to be with us and to be in us (Rom 8:31-39). His personal presence is both our greatest protection and our greatest resource. C. S. Lewis speaks about "God putting into us a bit of Himself. . . . He lends us a little of his reasoning powers and that is how we think; He puts a little of His love into us and that is how we love one another."[6]

Learning Christ's Wisdom

The sequence in Paul's thinking is clear. He is convinced that in Christ are "hidden all the treasures of wisdom and knowledge" so that no one may deceive "Christ's followers" by fine-sounding arguments (Col 2:3-4). Consequently, the responsibility for serious Christians is to access Jesus' mind and assimilate his "treasures of wisdom." Until followers of Jesus are able to think with the mind of Christ, they are vulnerable to the alluring invitations of the secular age.

Being a serious Christian is a summons to be a thoughtful person. Christians who faithfully love God with their minds pursue truth. They think about the faith, study the Bible, read significant books, listen to tapes, discuss ideas, reflect on implications of the gospel, take courses and specifically "develop their Christian minds."[7]

Rather than simply theorizing about the Christian mind and using "the mind of Christ" (1 Cor 2:16) to communicate God's truth in today's society, the better alternative is watching Jesus in action.

Encounters of the Creative Kind

We have already seen that Jesus adapted his communication to the circumstances of the person in his presence. He never said the same thing a second time. There is nothing in the biblical record to indicate he told anyone other than Nicodemus that "You must be born again" (Jn 3:1-15). His discussion with the Samaritan woman at the well was never repeated because there was only one woman with her particular scenario (Jn 4:1-20). In his encounter with Zacchaeus, Jesus talked tax and money because those issues were at the control center of Zacchaeus's life. Jesus' mind was tuned to the frequency of his audience. He was creative. In today's world, Jesus could excel as an advertising executive.

Jesus' same style of relating and communicating was evident in the way he recruited his disciples. After his baptism and experience with temptation in the desert, Jesus was walking beside the Sea of Galilee. He recognized Peter and his brother Andrew "casting a net into the lake, for they were fishermen." Jesus had recruiting on his mind and he said to them, "Come, follow me, and I will make you fishers of men" (Mk 1:16-18). Peter and Andrew gave up their trade and joined Jesus' cause.

When Jesus called Peter and Andrew to join his mission he was practicing the same principles he used with Zacchaeus. Instead of "tax talk" he spoke "fisher-ese." He used language and images that connected with their world. Jesus was not intending to provide a prototype for evangelism for all people for all time when he promised they would be fishers of men. Although this has been a frequent interpretation of this passage, we must recognize this reference to being "fishers of men" as Jesus' apt way of reaching fishermen.

Jesus' communication style extended beyond adapting his message to fit the circumstances of the person in his presence. In order to bring God's point of view into the situation, he keyed his responses to the subject matter being discussed. He was always prepared to tell the truth about all matters of life and death. The examples are numerous.

One day when Jesus and his disciples arrived at Capernaum, Jesus turned to his disciples and asked, "What were you arguing about on the road?" The disciples had been discussing who would be the greatest in the coming kingdom, and they were hesitant to respond. Jesus saw an opening for a moment of teaching and gathered the Twelve around him. "If anyone wants to be first, he must be the very last, and the servant of all" was his instruction (Mk 9:33-35).

In this case, the issue on the table was greatness, and Jesus took the opportunity to convey God's point of view on the subject. "If you want to be great, be a servant," was his reply.

One afternoon on a flight to the East Coast, I got into a conversation with a young man in his early thirties. I noted he was intently reading a book, but as he took a moment to gaze out the window I asked, "What are you reading?" He inserted the jacket cover to mark his page and handed the book to me. It was *Seeds of Greatness* by Dennis Waitley. I recognized the book as one of many that propagates the human-potential movement. We introduced ourselves to each other. His name was Greg.

Greg was very ready to talk about what he was reading. I commented that I had read a few books with a similar emphasis. We discovered that we had read a couple of the same titles. I asked him why he kept delving into the same area. He was candid. "Frankly, they encourage me to be all that I can be. I like their positive tone. They motivate me."

I asked, "Does Waitley have anything to say about being great when we serve the needs of other people?" Continuing, I said, "I know a teacher who believes that if you want to really be great, you need to be a servant."

Greg was intrigued. "Really," he said. "Who is this teacher?"

We spent the next hour talking—talking about Jesus, our inclinations to be self-centered, our resistance to being servants, what things stood in the way of our reaching our full potential and projecting what our world would be like if we lived out what Jesus taught.

At the very end of our conversation, Greg looked at me and insightfully asked, "Why is it that we are free to talk about sex in our society, but not about religion?"

My response was direct. "Greg, when we are talking about sex, we are talking about religion. God is concerned about our sex lives."

Greg smiled and said, "I'm going to think about that one."

The experience was stimulating and elevating for both of us.

The encounter with Greg was not a major event. It simply parallels what Jesus repeatedly modeled. He continually contextualized his communication. Jesus was both situation- and person-specific. He intentionally took advantage of situations to make his point and tell the truth about a wide range of concerns.

One day when Jesus had finished speaking, a Pharisee invited him home for a meal. Jesus accepted but failed to follow the legalistic practice to first wash before he began eating. The Pharisee communicated his surprise. In this situation, as in others with the Pharisees, Jesus was quick to take the offensive. "Now then, you Pharisees clean the outside of the cup and dish, but inside you are full of greed and wickedness" (Lk 11:39).

In another situation, Jesus was with a group of people when his mother and brothers arrived to see him. A messenger brought word to Jesus that members of his family wanted his attention. Setting the stage for his truth-telling, Jesus asked rhetorically, "Who are my mother and my brothers?" Then he looked at those seated in a circle around him and said, "Whoever does God's will is my brother and sister and mother" (Mk 3:31-35).

An interruption came while Jesus was speaking. "Teacher, tell my brother to divide the inheritance with me." Jesus' reply was direct but noncommittal, "Man, who appointed me a judge or an arbiter between you?" But in the moment, Jesus decided to take the incident a step further. "Watch out! Be on your guard against all kinds of greed." Jesus still wasn't finished. He added the profound principle that is as true today as it was then: "A man's life does not consist in the abundance of his possessions" (Lk 12:13-15).

Truth Frame of Reference

Jesus' mind was fully awake. He perceived questions as open doors to communicate his deeper agenda. Turning innocent conversations into significant discussions was a way of life for Jesus. He simply made his Father's ways known to the people who intersected his life. He responded to people around him with a *truth frame of reference*. Jesus was always ready to apply God's point of view to the subject at hand.

Too often, well-intentioned Christians limit their understanding of the gospel to a *cross frame of reference*. Particularly, when seeking to communicate a word of witness, they reduce the scope of God's truth to the parameters of John 3:16. The practice is not wrong, but it is narrow. Rather than engaging people in discussion that can go somewhere, it often shuts down communication and turns people away from the gospel.

Jesus' readiness to deal with a wide range of issues is an invitation for us to do the same. Many of the issues of life that Jesus addressed continue to be on today's agenda. At Samaria, Jesus raised the subject of sex with the woman at the well. The question of greatness and power was at the center of the debate with the disciples. Among the Pharisees, the discussion focused on the correlation between one's internal character and external behavior. We are still preoccupied with external appearances in these times. The other topics cited from Jesus' experience also remain as current concerns: Sabbath observance, the definition of "family" and the place of money in our lives.

As we follow Jesus' example, we will be able to speak God's truth in the natural flow of life with people in our world too.

There are specific subjects and areas of life that receive repeated and high-level attention in our society. Other topics may not be talked about openly, but they reside close to the surface of people's interests and concerns. Identifying and thinking through a Christian position on these matters will prepare us to take initiative and witness effectively when we have the opportunity.

For instance, in a society where views on sexual issues and lifestyles are perceived by the majority to be a realm for personal choice and individual preferences, simply making Christian pronouncements is not enough to win the day. At the same time, taking the posture "to live and let live" is an abdication of Christian responsibility. To this point in time, however, very few committed Christians have cultivated the art of having constructive conversations with people who hold different views on sexually related matters.

If Jesus were on earth today, without compromising his principles or alienating his audience, he would be able to engage in sexually related discussions that would be constructive and influential. When the Pharisees brought the woman caught in the act of adultery to him, Jesus was able to confront the issues and still diffuse the explosive situation. Jesus held to his principles. He also dealt seriously with the woman's sin and guilt. At the same time he demonstrated a compassionate spirit and protected the woman from being attacked by her accusers. But he also called both the guilty woman and her self-righteous accusers to be honest with themselves and to live with integrity. The Pharisees walked away reflective about their own sin. The woman walked away restored and forgiven for her past but also with the directive to "leave her life of sin." Jesus' stance offers us some guidelines for dealing with our present-day dilemmas (Jn 8:1-11).

For the sake of the gospel and in pursuit of an improved quality of life in society, we need to make progress in this area. We need to boldly represent the biblical sexual ethic that affirms heterosexual relationships in the context of marriage. Surely God wants us to represent him and gain back some of the ground that has been lost.

Mining the Mind of God

Several years ago I listened to a student address his peers on the subject of "Why I Am a Christian." Part of the way through his presentation he made this statement: "Christianity doesn't have all the answers, but it does have more answers than any other philosophical or religious system in the world." I agree with his analysis. As we study the Scriptures, augment our understanding with experience and input from other people and other sources, we can find a multitude of accurate answers to life's dilemmas, but not all the answers.

Unfortunately, many Christians project the mentality that the Bible is a treasure chest filled with inscribed golden coins. These well-meaning followers of Jesus relate to the people in their lives with the attitude that "if you have a problem, I will just reach into the chest and give you a golden coin that will solve it."

The Bible is more like a huge gold mine. Certainly there are golden nuggets to be discovered and treasured. But the full revelation of God is streamed throughout the Scriptures as veins of gold run through huge boulders. In order to get the full mind of God on complex issues, like sexuality, the Word of God has to be mined.

God has made his ways known on the issues of famine, economic disparity, lotteries, unemployment, racial discrimination, apartheid, genetic engineering, pornography, unwed mothers and the use of tissue from aborted babies. Through persistent study and discussions with others we can discover God's thoughts on issues of concern and need. Mining the mind of God is an arduous and complex task. It is a lifetime endeavor. But it is worth our most noble pursuit.

In the end, "either God exists and thereby guarantees life's meaning and wholeness, or else God does not exist, religion is irrelevant, and life falls apart. Too often these alternatives get mixed up: people who believe God exists either think of religion as peripheral to the life that absorbs them or else look on 'secular' things as peripheral to their religion. Even the modern religious man has lost the religious unity of life."[8]

The people of God who pay the price of mining for God's truth receive the reward of becoming whole people. Their lives move toward unity. Instead of suffering from life-denying fragmentation, they taste the richness of integration. More and more, they put the pieces of life together in a coherent whole. And more and more often, they have increased opportunities to speak the truth of God as it applies to a wide range of issues and concerns.

Measuring Our Effectiveness

A couple of years ago, Wendall shared an incident with me about his ministry among business people. God was helping him make a wide range of contacts with executive types, and he was discovering a number of people who were open to the gospel. One of his big obstacles was finding enough time to get together with busy people. Wendall was especially pleased when an upper-level executive, who was actively investigating the faith, invited him on an overnight business trip. The man specifically said he had a long list of questions about Christianity that were troubling him.

The night before they were to leave, Wendall had a family emergency that made it impossible for him to take the trip. He was deeply disappointed. However, he quickly put together plan *b*. He had a ministry colleague who had met the businessman on a previous occasion. Wendall called his business friend, explained his situation and made the arrangements for his colleague to take the trip in his place.

When they returned, Wendall received two accounts about the significance of the trip. His colleague thought the time was effective. They had had hours to talk together, God was the center of attention and "I was able to share my testimony."

When Wendall asked his business friend, "How did the time go?" there was a different response, "Oh, it was all right, I guess. But the trouble was, your friend was a one-way thinker. All he could do was talk about God."

There is a significant difference between talking about God and telling God's truth. Witnessing effectively is not just dispensing information. It is making meaning out of the whole of life, being a meaning maker. In this age, as followers of Jesus communicate God's truth about life's current concerns—as well as the significance of Christ's death and resurrection—the gospel will become a viable option for more people who are not yet Christians.

Chapter Nine

TRANSCENDING WORDS

TELLING *GOD'S TRUTH IS ONE THING.* DOING *HIS* truth is another. In our "information society," even when carefully chosen words are spoken in the right way at the right time, very few people will be prompted to believe in Jesus and follow him on the basis of words alone. Words in today's world are like worn-out batteries—they have been overused and drained of their power.

Can words be recharged? Can they speak with power again?

In this age, "show me" rather than "tell me" reflects the temperament of the times. Consequently, words that faithfully communicate the claims of the gospel will only ring true when those who *say* the truth *do* the truth with the deeds of their lives.

The state of our culture complements Jesus' emphasis in the Sermon on the Mount: "Not everyone who says to me, 'Lord, Lord,' will enter the kingdom of heaven, but only he who does the will of my Father who is in heaven" (Mt 7:21).

Word Weary

The five-pound weekend newspapers, the unending stream of junk mail, computerized personal letters that aren't really personal, news and weather for twenty-four hours a day on television, unread magazines, crammed book stores with too many acclaimed best sellers and the never-ending public opinion polls have left us dazed. Our mental systems are on overload. And the excessive information has conditioned us not to believe or respond.

Our world is weary of words.

Too often, people who matter to us have let us down. We believed their verbal promises. But their words turned out to be cheap payments for expensive experiences. They said, "You can count on me. I'll be there when you need me." But then they weren't there. Life isn't perfect, we know, but broken promises still hurt. We become suspicious that people don't really mean what they say. Our suspicions breed a spirit of skepticism. We continue to hear the words but inside we think, "I'll wait and see."

Protective business procedures are now replacing what used to be left to an honor system. Even in first-class hotels, a person's word is not trusted. A common practice is for a member of the housekeeping staff to come to the door and ask, "Did you use the minibar last night?" Even when you answer with a definitive, "No, I didn't have anything," an actual count is made anyway as you stand there. In many North American cities, it is mandatory to first pay the attendant for your gasoline before you put it into the tank of your car. Their history with people who say one thing but do another is forcing organizations to put insulting systems in place in order to counter increasing mistrust.

In the religious realm, we have been let down too. High-profile preachers have breached our trust. More than just one or two have been guilty of the worst kind of perverted religious exhibitionism. We don't want to hear any more bad news, but still we wonder if those we want to trust are really trustworthy. Have they also deceived us with words that don't match their actions?

Today, actions mean more than words. What are some of the consequences for evangelism for living in a culture that is weary of words? In previous decades, appealing to reason and using apologetic arguments was an effective prod to awaken people's minds and convince them to believe. When people were more interested in resolving the meaning of life, offering reasons for faith in Christ often prompted people to reflect and then respond. But the demotion of words has led to a loss of confidence in ideas and reason.

Money above Meaning

A new approach is needed now. The cultural mood is changing, as Bobby McFerrin brilliantly captured with his hit song, "Don't Worry, Be Happy."

For the past twenty years, researchers at the University of California in Los Angeles have surveyed the values and life goals of college freshmen. "Although many of the value statements have waxed and waned in popularity since the 1960s, two of the items have shown especially consistent and contrasting trends. The item showing the strongest upward trend is 'being well off financially.' ... The value showing the most precipitous decline in student endorsement is 'developing a meaningful philosophy of life.' "[1] From the late sixties into the second half of the eighties, the value ascribed to "being well off financially" increased dramatically from 40% to 70%. During the same period of time, the importance of "developing a meaningful philosophy of life" declined progressively from over 80% down to 43%.

The trend toward a decrease in the concern to "develop a meaningful philosophy of life" correlates with other research that reveals a low value for intelligence itself.[2] There is evidence to conclude that the inclination to think about life is being pushed aside by the desire to experience life. The gravitational pull is more toward titillating the senses rather than stimulating the mind.

Relativism has also dulled the cutting edge of reason. The rational has been pushed aside by the appeal of the relational. The ache to be loved has propelled the realm of the heart over the realm of the head. The place of the objective has been overruled by the subjective. In the cultural milieu, the demand to be tolerant and open has reduced the persuasive influence of truth. These trends have direct implications for evangelism.

Going beyond Expectations

This is the cultural condition in which committed Christians are challenged to make Jesus news again. One thing is certain—if the gospel is just the articulation of more words, the consequences of Christ's death and resurrection will remain nothing more than a historical event. However, if God's people can translate the theory of their words into lifestyles that are distinctively Christian, the power of the gospel will be seen. And today, seeing is what leads to believing.

Jesus' teaching in Matthew 5:43-47 speaks directly to the need and predicament of our times.

> You have heard that it was said, "Love your neighbor and hate your enemy." But I tell you: Love your enemies and pray for those who persecute you, that you may be sons of your Father in heaven. . . . If you love those who love you, what reward will you get? Are not even the tax collectors doing that? And if you greet only your brothers, what are you doing more than others? Do not even pagans do that?

Jesus sets a higher standard for those who claim to be his followers than he expects from tax collectors and pagans who belong to the world. Being hospitable to people who like you may be a nice gesture, but the behavior has more to do with social grace than distinctive

Christian living. Loving those who love you conforms to the natural laws of life. Loving and praying for your enemies is the standard for members of the family of God. Reflecting the consensus of social codes in the culture may be commendable, but it is not necessarily Christian. Jesus is clear. Being the same as sinners is not good enough for those who claim to be committed to him.

C. S. Lewis rightly contends that "if conversion to Christianity makes no improvement in a man's outward actions—if he continues to be just as snobbish or spiteful or envious or ambitious as he was before—then I think we must suspect that his 'conversion' was largely imaginary: and after one's original conversion, every time one thinks one has made an advance, that is the test to apply. Fine feelings, new insights, greater interest in 'religion' mean nothing unless they make our actual behaviour better."[3]

In another place Jesus gathered his disciples together and spoke further about how Christians are to be distinctive:

> You know that those who are regarded as rulers of the Gentiles lord it over them, and their high officials exercise authority over them. Not so with you. Instead, whoever wants to become great among you must be your servant, and whoever wants to be first must be slave of all. For even the Son of Man did not come to be served, but to serve, and to give his life as a ransom for many. (Mk 10:42-45)

God's people are different. What the world condones is not adequate for Jesus' followers. And on the subject of greatness, compared to how the world lives, kingdom values are upside-down.

The picture Jesus paints for his disciples is to live life with one hand clasped in the hand of God and the other reaching out to serve the needs of others. Part of what it means for us to become a new creature in Christ Jesus is to embody what Jesus practiced. It is to have the soul of a servant transplanted into our human frame. Rather than defining greatness in terms of power and authority over others, for the Christian, greatness is relinquishing self-interest and the pursuit of personal ambition so the needs of others can be served.

In his superb book *Servant Leadership,* Robert Greenleaf describes the posture of a servant in the context of being a leader. He contends that "the servant leader is servant first. . . . That person is sharply different from one who is leader first. . . . The difference manifests itself in the care taken by the servant—first to make sure that other people's highest priority needs are being served. The best test is—do those being served grow as persons? Do they, while being served, become healthier, wiser, freer, more autonomous, more likely themselves to become servants?"[4]

Knowing the Value of People

A readiness to live with a servant spirit not only depends on the presence of God in one's life, it rests on the cornerstone of bestowing a high value on people.

I read a short newspaper account about the complications in rescuing an injured mountain climber in South America. The statement was brief: "A seriously injured Canadian climber had to lie on the side of a South American mountain for five days while a friend arranged to pay the government $18,000 in advance for his rescue." When a Christian value system is in charge of decision-making, human worth diminishes other concerns. When a mountain climber's life is at risk, a Christlike response is to rescue first and worry about paying later.

A revealing test of how we value people is indicated by the manner in which we treat the children in our lives. The test is a valid indicator because children are not just the little people in our society, they are the weak people. They do not have leverage to establish their own status. They are dependent creatures. Children often get grouped with others in society who are considered "disadvantaged." Children are powerless. They are in no position to fight for themselves. In order to be deemed valuable, they must be granted value from the adults in their lives. Unless children are bestowed with dignity by the older people who share their world, they are subjected to demeaning treatment. In a world where we often hear of abandoned and abused children, valuing and loving the little ones among us is testimony that we see them as precious creations of God.

My wife Beth recently observed a mother and her toddler daughter walking across a shopping mall parking lot. What made them stand out was that they held hands as they walked and talked together. For a few steps they skipped along and then both giggled. The stroll across the pavement was more like an event than just a short walk. When the two of them reached the car, the mother lifted her daughter up so she could sit on the hood. They talked for a short moment while the mother unlocked and opened the car door. She returned to her prized possession, gave her a hug and then helped her daughter with the seat belt. "The child was definitely not a bag of groceries," my wife said.

Parents are entitled to their quota of bad days. The routine pressures of life prevent most casual strolls from being turned into permanent memories. However, when it comes to the true value that we place or do not place on people, one test question remains: "How do we treat children?"

Generosity of Money and Soul
Another indicator that makes loud announcements about the value we inherently ascribe to people revolves around decisions we make about money.

A friend named Anne recently sold her small business. Her interests were purchased by a former employee. Negotiations were conducted in an honest and forthright manner. Extraordinary efforts were made to clarify the status of the outstanding payables and receivables.

The nature of the business meant that, of necessity, a few matters were left in a transitional state. Anne made specific mention of a commission check that was clearly payment for her work prior to signing the agreement of sale.

A few weeks after the transaction was complete, the commission check arrived at Anne's old office. When she inquired about the money in question, the new owner sent signals that she felt the check belonged to her. Anne's inner spirit was sent into turmoil. She was a Christian. What should she do?

A couple of days later, with clear resolve in her mind, Anne went back to her old business to deal with the troublesome matter. She sat across the desk from her former employee and began the discussion by simply saying, "My friend, our relationship is more important than the check. If you feel the money is rightfully yours, I want you to have it. My spirit is clear about that." But in the end, the new owner refused to accept the check.

Cheapskates make lousy Christians! They also score low on the servanthood scale.

A generation ago, Jackie Robinson was the first black man to play major-league baseball. Although he was an all-star caliber player, he was insulted and demeaned with constant racial harassment. One day during a Brooklyn Dodgers game in Cincinnati, the racial taunting reached a crescendo. Fellow player Pee Wee Reese had seen and heard enough. White and popular, Reese turned to the umpire and called a time out. Slowly and deliberately, Reese walked over toward Robinson and physically put his arm around his shoulder. The two men stood together for a long moment. The brave act made a loud announcement to the crowd. Without words, Reese boldly proclaimed to the jeering fans, "We are two human beings. Jackie Robinson is my friend."[5]

During President Carter's administration when several American diplomats were held hostage in Iran, the significance of responding to others in a tangible manner was underscored in a different way. One of the prisoners kept his food ration to share with the other hostages when they would come to visit him. *Time* magazine observed that "a jail cell was turned into a hospitality center."

Concrete behavior is more potent than mere words. *Doing* the truth is more persuasive than *saying* the truth. Deeds transcend words. Although words without deeds may be true, particularly in this age, they are weak.

Haircuts, Hamburgers and Houses

My own spirit is stimulated whenever I see the people of God practicing the theory of their Christian convictions.

Darren is a street evangelist in a midsized western city. He has been a Christian for less than two years and will soon be twenty-five years old. Christ had radically changed his life, and he simply believed that Jesus would transform other people too. I asked him, "What do you do on the streets?"

"Well, I hang around. I talk with people. I'm really interested in seeing young people out there come to Christ, but it's a hard life on the street. At first, I was just into witnessing . . . telling the street kids about Jesus. Lately, I'm doing more than talking. I may meet a kid who hasn't had a haircut for six months and after I know him a little bit, I make the offer to take him to this barber I know. He gives me a cut rate for my clients!

"The other thing I'm doing is buying my street friends a lot of hamburgers. People are hungry out there. Over a hot meal I try to work the conversation around to God and his desire to help them get into a better way of living."

Joanne is a young woman with a tender heart. She is a serious Christian and a recent university graduate finding her way in the work world. Through a former student friend now living in another city, she got connected with fifteen-year-old Heather.

When Joanne first met Heather, the teen-ager was alone and pregnant, the father of the child having abandoned the situation. During long evening conversations mixed with tears and emotional outbursts, the two women worked through the decision of whether or not Heather should have an abortion. They both concluded that the best option was to carry the baby to full term. During the following months, Heather spent most of her days and nights eating and sleeping at

Joanne's place. In Joanne's words, "You can't just tell people what to do without being committed to hang in there with them."

I was meeting with a businessman named Spencer who gives God the credit for blessing him with many prosperous business opportunities. We discovered that we had several shared acquaintances, and Spencer brought me up to date on the affairs of a family I have known and appreciated for years.

The family in question have spent their whole life serving faithfully in small church situations. Circumstances have prevented them from owning their own home, and retirement is only a few years away. As casually as you would ask someone to "Please pass the salt" at mealtime, Spencer said, "You will be interested in knowing that yesterday I made it possible for your friends to move into their own home."

Deeds are indeed a powerful testimony to our God. But while we witness to our God when we live distinctively Christian lives, there is a flip side to this truth. Our foolish and unloving actions also reflect on our God. I know of a woman named Yvonne, who, after her husband had left her with two children for another woman, was told by her pastor that her "presence is unhealthy for the marriages of the people in our church." Today, Yvonne is no longer a participant in any church and she continues to wonder if God really is in this world.

Embracing someone who is being publicly jeered, sharing your food rations, paying for haircuts and hamburgers for street people, giving up your personal time, opening both the door of your life and your apartment, and writing checks for large amounts without even getting a tax-deductible receipt—these are not glamorous activities, but they are godly. Our world desperately needs more people who call themselves followers of Jesus to live life like Darren, Joanne and Spencer.

Calloused Hands versus a Calloused Heart
While it is rewarding and worthwhile, living the life of a servant will also get you involved in untidy situations. Servant-style living will guar-

antee callouses on your hands, though never on your heart.

Helping people move from one apartment to another is not often the most pleasant way to spend a Saturday afternoon. Driving older people to doctor appointments, baby-sitting children for single mothers, teaching international students how to use the transit system, volunteering at a food bank, collecting for a charity, visiting the sick, encouraging the discouraged and generally surrendering oneself to the needs of others takes willful and methodical determination. Like it or not, being a Christian and serving others is a call to a ministry of inconvenience.

I remember the day Jeff appeared at my door. He had a gift in his hand. Jeff had been a member of one of my discipleship groups when he was a university student. We had not seen each other for a couple of years. During that time, he had graduated and spent a year traveling through a number of countries in South America. He had just arrived home.

Jeff's gift was a pound of coffee. Along with an explanation, he handed me a package that had obviously been on a long journey. "When I was in Colombia about six months ago, I got thinking about you and remembered how much you enjoyed a good cup of coffee. I also thought about the helpful times our discipleship group had together. I just wanted to say, 'Thank you.' "

I was staggered by his kindness. My spirit was overwhelmed with the realization that he had carried a pound of coffee in his backpack for the last six months. Something in me wanted to save the tattered package and its contents as some kind of memorial, a symbolic tribute to the deeper meaning of gift-giving.

The Christian commitment to others stands in contrast with the normative standards in today's world. How many people would have carried a one-pound thank-you note on their back for six months? No, the dominant drive in modern society is to seek convenience. It is to cater to personal desires and affirm self-interest. The shocking reality is that unless the people of God resist the prevailing orientation of the culture, they will begin adopting the ways of the world as their own.

Jesus' radical teaching of the importance of serving the needs of others first should help us counter that tendency. His message implicitly exclaims, "It is far better to have calloused hands than a calloused heart."

Ready to Give

If we are serious about living as Jesus lived, being both psychologically and practically prepared to give will be a natural part of our Christian posture.

I know a man named Sven who began to learn this lesson early one morning on a public bus as he made his way toward another day of school. He was seated at the back of the bus in what he called his "morning daze."

The ride was normal and uneventful until an older woman got on the bus who couldn't speak English. Neither was she aware of how much she had to pay for the fare. The bus driver was not having one of his better days. He kept repeating, "One dollar—put the money in the box." The woman simply didn't understand what to do and she stood there shrugging her shoulders. By this time the driver was virtually shouting at the woman and he announced, "I'm not moving this bus until you pay your money."

Many of the other passengers on the bus decided they would vote with the driver and they also started hollering at the woman. A few of the riders were actually swearing at the woman who by this time was confused and paralyzed. The commotion finally brought Sven to his senses and he quickly computed someone had to rescue the poor woman. He dug into his pocket to find a dollar and made his way toward the front of the bus. Without saying a word, he dropped the single dollar bill into the box and offered his arm to the older woman. The bus began to move again.

And Darren, the man who pays for haircuts and hamburgers, was himself the recipient of this kind of spontaneous giving. Several of us were sitting around a table as he talked about his street ministry. An older woman in the circle was particularly captivated by Darren and his desire to help those we label "dropouts." In a quiet and natural manner, she reached into her purse and took out a folded one-hundred-dollar bill that she kept for such occasions. With a smile on her face, she reached across the table and pressed the bill into Darren's hand with the statement, "I love what you are doing. Here's a little something for a few more haircuts and maybe even a steak or two."

I suspect that within the next day or two that same woman folded up another one-hundred-dollar bill so she could be prepared to give again.

Carrying some money in a secret place for the express purpose of looking for a situation to give it away is not only honorable, in today's world it is distinctively Christian. The amount is not really the issue. It may be $1, $5, $20, $50 or $100. Living with an attitude that desires to respond is what really matters. Opportunities to act will abound.

Restoring Word Power

The Scriptures raise the troublesome question, "Salt is good, but if it loses its saltiness, how can it be made salty again?" (Lk 14:34). The same predicament exists with words in today's world. "Words are good, but when words have lost their power, how can they be empowered again?"

Some churches live with the disposition that being a Christian is a matter of saying the right words. Their Bible teaches, "Well *said,* good and faithful servant. . . . Come and share your master's happiness." Other Christian orientations emphasize the importance of understanding God's truth and embracing right doctrine. Their Bible teaches, "Well *understood,* good and faithful servant. . . . Come and share your master's happiness." In the parable of the talents, Jesus assesses the record of the five-talent and two-talent men and announces, "Well *done,* good and faithful servant. . . . Come and share your master's happiness" (Mt 25:21).

When deeds are wedded to our words, our Christian witness is more believable. It's like the salt which makes good food taste even better. It brings out the flavor. Salt also makes people thirsty. And seeing the Christian life lived out in a servant style will not only make people thirsty for the "water of life," but our words will be empowered again.

Pastor Frank Tillapaugh, in his book *Unleashing Your Potential,* comments on the church that understands this principle and on the one that doesn't. "If a church retains an average atmosphere where people are expected to pray, read the Bible and live holy lives . . . then not much is likely to happen." On the other hand, when the gospel is understood as both words and deeds, and God's people are stimulated to dream, then the gospel streams into life. "Over the years dreamers in our church have been used by God to conceive, establish and run a host of ministries. . . . In that freewheeling climate, a street school, medical clinic, Christian mediation service and ministries in the following areas have been developed: step-families, cults, jail, street refugees, senior adults, physically disabled, alcoholics and more."[6]

People who minister to international students understand that the way to empower words is to combine them with acts of service. While respecting and accepting what other world religions teach, the people of God who have fruitful ministries among internationals specialize in hospitality. They begin by meeting their new foreign friends at the airport and helping with the heavy suitcases. They help find apartments, give city tours, stand in registration lines, interpret what is meant by strange sayings and generally cultivate the art of helping people feel comfortable in a foreign land. Their acts of love and service are not a set-up for Bible study, retreats and prayer meetings. They are acts of unconditional love for the sake of lifting the level of life in the name of Christ for people who have specific needs.

But international ministry has its own challenges. Penetrating the

Muslim world with the gospel has been a tough task. Ray Bakke details the experience of a businessman who became a missionary in Indonesia. After moving his family into a slum area in Surabaya and building his home out of crates like everyone else, he figured out that deeds had to precede words. Surrounded by devout Muslims, the businessman began asking his well-off friends for donations and then he called the men of the community together. "My Christian friends want you to have this money to build your mosque" was his surprise offer. He then spent "the next six months helping them to build the mosque. He began a Bible study with the people with whom he worked, and eventually thirty adult believers had been baptized, with thirty teenagers coming to afternoon classes."[7]

Doing the will of God in today's world will seed the possibility that God exists in ways that really matter. Christians who not only talk the faith but walk the faith will be perceived as plausible people. They will be a threat to the conventional conclusions in the modern world that God is unnecessary. Without making verbal announcements, the way they live will make people around them wonder why they are different. When people see tangible evidence of the influence of God in those who make religious faith claims, some who see the fruit of faith will be compelled to search for God themselves.

Telling God's truth and doing God's truth are meant to be two parts of a whole. And when they do stand together, the church of Christ is not only built up, it has credibility in the eyes of the world.

Chapter Ten

HELPING
PEOPLE
DECIDE

GOD CALLS PEOPLE TO HIMSELF WITH A PERSONAL TOUCH. Everyone has a unique story to tell.

Cynthia became a Christian when she was invited to join a neighborhood Bible study. At the same time, her marriage was in a major crisis. One morning as she was vacuuming her carpets, with an emotional mix inside her that made tears stream down her face, she looked to God and literally shouted out, "If you are up there, please help me!" In Cynthia's words, "Something happened to me in that moment. My inside world started to calm down. I sensed that God had touched me." Today, Cynthia leads Bible studies in her own home.

Nolan's story is totally different. He was a member of the counter-culture who spent two memorable years wandering from one experience to another under the guise of "looking for himself." While hitchhiking one afternoon, Nolan was picked up by a group of people driving a brightly painted "hippie van." Within a few miles it was evident to Nolan that the other passengers in the van were "religious types." Before long he was introduced to the contents of a booklet entitled, "The Four Spiritual Laws." A couple of hours later, Nolan parted company with his fellow hippie passengers. As he tells his story, "I was parked with my pack by the side of the road waiting for another ride when I reached into my pocket, and there was that booklet. I read it through again and somehow it made sense to me. I've traveled with God since that momentous day."

Stephanie was one of those well-adjusted, polite college students who do not seem to need to be "saved" from anything. But then she received a roommate, Sarah, who turned out to be petty and vindictive. "I find that I am now thinking of ways to get even with Sarah," she said as we talked. "I honestly didn't know that I was capable of the evil that has entered my mind. I think I need God." She became a Christian soon after.

For every person who is able to articulate the specific circumstances of his or her conversion, there is undoubtedly an equal number who do not have an awareness of when they came to faith. For them, the journey to belief in Christ transpires over an undefinable period of time. They simply know that Christ is a real part of their existence and they are seeking to live out the theory of their faith in their daily walk in this world.

No one encounters Christ on their own. Almost always, other Christians are involved. So the question we must answer is, "What is the human role in helping people decide to become followers of Jesus?

Complement God's Work
The complexity of the question defies a simple response. However,

in a general sense, our primary role in influencing others to become Christians is to complement what God is already doing. It is to be in partnership with the activity of the Holy Spirit.

God is the one with the prerogative and power to redeem and forgive. God and God only is the one who saves and restores. At best, the human role only complements the divine activity. In his final days on earth, Jesus spoke definitively about the role of the Holy Spirit in God's plan of salvation: "It is for your good that I am going away. Unless I go away, the Counselor will not come to you. . . . When he comes, he will convict the world of guilt in regard to sin and right- eousness and judgment" (Jn 16:7-8).

Accordingly, there is no salvation without God's initiative. The Holy Spirit sensitizes people's consciences to sin and its consequences. Unless the Spirit convicts, God's voice is unheard.

With equal clarity, the Scriptures also mandate a human role in writing the salvation story. Jesus said to his disciples:

> All authority in heaven and on earth has been given to me. There- fore go and make disciples of all nations, baptizing them in the name of the Father and of the Son and of the Holy Spirit, and teaching them to obey everything I have commanded you. (Mt 28:18-19)

And in the Acts of the Apostles, we read Jesus' parting words to his disciples: "You will receive power when the Holy Spirit comes on you; and you will be my witnesses" (Acts 1:8).

God is clearly committed to a team approach in calling his es- tranged creation back into fellowship with himself. Like one of the elements in a chemical formula which needs all its ingredients to work, the human contribution is a critical component in the drama that prompts people to confess their sin and place their confidence in Christ.

In Jesus' commissioning of the apostle Paul, we again see how Jesus asks us to cooperate with his work and mission:

> I am sending you to them to open their eyes and turn them from

darkness to light, and from the power of Satan to God, so that they may receive forgiveness of sins and a place among those who are sanctified by faith in me. (Acts 26:17-18)

Jesus' commissioning of Paul was given at a strategic time in the development of the early church. Jesus' clear directive to Paul enabled Paul to claim "I was not disobedient to the vision from heaven" (Acts 26:19).

Although Jesus' mandate for Paul was set at a unique time and circumstance, the dynamics of helping people leave their own ways and return to the family of God remain the same today. When the principles Jesus revealed to Paul are practiced in today's world, the modern church will see changed lives and an expanded, enlivened church.

Our Commission

We are all a part of Jesus' great mission to "make disciples of all nations." Wherever we are, we are to live and preach the good news to others. As followers of their risen Lord, loyal disciples have repeatedly and deliberately accepted Jesus' mission as their own. They have said yes to the assignment Jesus has delegated to them. They have intentionally lived and proclaimed God's good news to people who share their racial bloodlines. They have served people who are close to them. Others have left their homes and families and the cultures where they were comfortable in order to lift up Jesus where he was unknown.

One of the great temptations for committed Christians in North America is to believe in Jesus but to live without any sense of sharing his mission. The temptation is especially real because most people in our society live without a commitment to a cause that is beyond the range of their personal goals. Christians have a higher calling than to simply funnel their energy and gifts into the container of their personal pursuits. To believe in Jesus is also to be sent—sent with the good news of the gospel to those who are near and sometimes to those who are far away.

The primary vehicle through which Christ's mission is accomplished is the church. The church is a place to join with others who want to know God's ways and be nurtured in the faith. As a corporate entity, the church equips her people to live faithfully in the world. Being a participant in a community puts a check on individual excesses. But most importantly the church exists "to prepare God's people for works of service, so that the body of Christ may be built up until we all reach unity in the faith and in the knowledge of the Son of God and become mature" (Eph 4:12).

In God's game plan, the church does not exist to serve her own organizational needs. Rather, the resources of the church are to be used, first, to build up the people of God and then to deploy those same people to take the mission of Christ into the world. The church exists for mission. A missionless church is reduced to an activity center for members only. The church of Jesus Christ does serve the wide-ranging needs of her members, but she also mobilizes her members into her Savior's mission.

From Darkness to Light

When Jesus was on earth, in a discussion about spiritual blindness with his disciples, he frankly stated that the unspiritual do not have the secrets of the kingdom of heaven (Mt 13:11). Jesus went on to explain by quoting from the prophet Isaiah: "This people's heart has become calloused; they hardly hear with their ears, and they have closed their eyes. Otherwise they might see with their eyes, hear with their ears, understand with their hearts and turn, and I would heal them" (Mt 13:15).

The challenge of revealing the "secrets of the kingdom" to people with closed eyes and calloused hearts is most often a slow process.

People who become followers of Jesus and stay committed to him for the long term often move toward Christian belief step by step and stage by stage. They crawl out of the darkness of the night, spend time, sometimes considerable time, lurking in the shadows of the early morning light before they eventually stride into the brightness of a sunny day.

God is not a member of a traveling circus performing religious magic. He does not have a special wand that he uses to zap people when they project a little faith in his direction. Certainly, conversion is a miracle, but the biblical motif for salvation is not the theatrical plot that unravels its complexity in a single evening. Real life is not so neatly packaged.

Too many overzealous evangelists believe in microwave evangelism. The influence of our instant society and the driving urge to call people to an immediate decision for Christ have combined to produce "impatient evangelism." Consequently, some people who have been methodically walking out of darkness into light have been shoved into the kingdom—many of them prematurely. Unfortunately, those who have been pressed into the kingdom too soon usually stay for only a short visit rather than taking up permanent residence.

Coming into a genuine relationship with Christ is a profound, life-changing experience. Conversion to Christ reorders the whole of life: God is restored to his rightful place, the focus of worship and praise; the self is released from tyrannizing egotism and freed to become a constructive part of a community; values are scrutinized and restructured; motives are energized; morals and ethics are raised to a level that is truly human; one's heart is sensitized to the needs of others; one's mind is elevated to think more noble thoughts and pursue that which is good and true; one's hands are extended out to the world and lifted up to the Redeemer.

How can such a transformation be trivialized? Why would anyone cheapen the richness of encountering Christ by selling fraudulent, no-cost, quick-fix faith? What would justify pushing people into the kingdom when they are not ready to willingly respond to the overtures of the God of the universe?

Another way of thinking about people who are in the process of becoming Christians is to picture them on God's time clock. If twelve o'clock represents the time for a decision to believe in Jesus, then it follows that people on their way to faith are somewhere else on the clock. Those who are just beginning to see Christianity as a legitimate alternative are back at one or two o'clock. Those who are nearing a decision to accept Christ are at ten or eleven o'clock. An important part of witnessing effectively is to determine where people are on God's clock. Accordingly, when people are at three o'clock, a significant step toward becoming a Christian would be helping them move to four o'clock.

The stakes in the spiritual struggle are so high and so consequential that choosing between Satan and God deserves a clear-cut, deliberate decision. Faithful witnessing is engaging people in a manner that prompts them to turn from less darkness to more light. It is cooperating with God's activity and his timing. It is assisting people to proceed from six o'clock to seven o'clock on the way to hearing the chimes ring at high noon when Christ and his salvation are received and celebrated.

Witnessing as a Life Skill

One responsibility the corporate church must accept is to equip her people to witness faithfully and appropriately in today's world. Otherwise, the mission of the church will not only be curtailed, it will be contained within the community that is already Christian.

We often turn witnessing (that is, partnering with God to open blind eyes and turn people from darkness to light) into an ordeal by simply not doing it. Sometimes fear holds us back. In other instances, we confuse passiveness toward God as disinterest and assume that people have already decided that God is not for them. Many people who attend church regularly want to participate in Christ's mission but for various reasons their lips are sealed and their lives are silent.

Those who have the desire to move out of silence will be helped to realize that, like many other things in life, witnessing is a learned skill. As we journey through life, we learn to do many different things.

Our acquired skills may range from driving a car to playing tennis, from baking bread to building houses, from designing computer software to teaching the Bible. The combination of our abilities, the level of instruction we receive and how frequently we practice what we have learned largely determine the level of our expertise.

Learning to engage others in spiritually related discussions is similar to acquiring other skills. Just as there are rules of the road for driving a car, there are social codes to follow when presenting God's ways to people. Taking tennis lessons from someone who plays the game well and knows how to teach is helpful. Likewise, spending time with people who have experience in witnessing is also beneficial. Just as a builder works from an architect's plan, interacting with people with a clear model in mind is also wise. But in the end, we develop the ability to communicate God's truth and care for people's needs by doing it. As we practice, we are bound to improve. Like any skill, once we have learned to witness appropriately, we make decisions about how often we will speak or act.

The difficulty for many people who have made attempts to learn to witness is that they theorize without practicing. They go to seminars to be told what to do, but for many reasons the doing doesn't get done. By itself, the seminar approach to learning to witness is as effective as taking swimming lessons by correspondence without ever getting into the water. Certainly, God's people need to be taught how to witness, but the far greater need is simply to start doing what we already know God wants us to do.

Engage to Transform

My invitation to you in this book is to study the culture as well as the Bible as you figure out how to witness and faithfully follow Jesus in these times. Richard Niebuhr, in his classic book *Christ and Culture*, helps Christians both set their attitude toward the modern culture and anticipate what God wants to do in today's world. Niebuhr suggests four ways to view the relationship between Christ and culture:[1]

Christ against culture. In this view Christ opposes what is in the world, and a clear choice must be made between the two alternatives. The culture is hopelessly depraved. The Christian then has no real choice but to abandon what cannot be salvaged. Separation from the evil world is the obvious strategy. Abdication and disengagement from the culture is the only real godly option.

Christ of culture. The second view is the antithesis of the first. Instead of Christ and culture being radically different from each other, they are closely identified with each other. There is remarkable agreement or overlap between life according to the kingdom of God and life in the modern culture. Jesus is considered to not only be a legitimate historical figure but is also a contemporary hero. This view invites Christians to blend into the world and to be assimilated by making the world's ways their own.

Christ above culture. The third view divides Christ and culture into sacred and secular categories. Life of the spirit and life of the world are disconnected from each other. A dualism exists. On the one hand there is the authority of Christ, and on the other hand there is the authority of the state. Both exist, and without accommodation both are somehow to be obeyed. Christians who adopt this orientation will be forced to compartmentalize their faith from the rest of their lives. Having a personal faith without the necessity of a public Christian presence will be acceptable.

Christ transforming culture. Niebuhr labels this view the "conversionist solution." Christ is the converter, the transformer of what is fallen and perverted. This understanding is "modeled on the Incarnation. It does not deny that the culture needs to be changed, but it does not flinch from engagement."² This last option invites Christians to not only enter the secular world but to challenge it with the expectation that God will transform and *re*create what he created in the first place.

Clearly, the view that Christ transforms culture is the biblical position for living in a society that is secularizing itself away from God and his concerns. The strategy must not be to run from the world but rather to engage the world, to interact in a bold but compassionate manner with what is happening in modern society.

Engaging the culture will take many different forms. It will occur again and again at interpersonal levels. Sometimes issues will be raised in more open forums. The religious legacy in North America, which has so effectively blended culture and Christianity, will present many situations where people who live in a manner that is consistent with their convictions will have opportunities to engage and transform the world around them.

Principles of Pluralism

No one can dispute the fact that a multicultural, secularized and pluralistic society is complex. Whether we are serious Christians or not, we must all learn to respect each other's beliefs and live with each other's differences. Evangelistic endeavors that are effective in today's world will be marked with an understanding of the principles that govern a pluralistic society:

Acceptance of diversity. Many ways of thinking and living are the norm in a society that is pluralistic. Tolerance is a virtue. In order to preserve one's rights and privileges, others in the society have to be given the same rights and privileges. Diversity is a reality of life to be accepted. Personal rights are subject to the limits of what society concludes to be best for the common good.

Appreciation of options. Giving someone else the prerogative to make choices about what they believe inherently gives one permission to make one's own belief choices. Living with an attitude that makes an honest attempt to appreciate what other people believe invites understanding and fosters mutual respect between people. When people respect each other, it is not necessary to always agree in order to cultivate significant relationships.

Interaction with alternatives. The tolerance factor that is built into pluralism is an open opportunity for evangelism. When people are locked into closed systems, they are beyond the reach of new thoughts and ideas. By contrast, when people sense they are accepted and appreciated for who they are, they are ready to interact without being defensive.

When the principles of pluralism are embodied in attitude and action, a wholesome environment is created for presenting the gospel. The results are then in God's hands. Our confidence rests in the power of God's truth and the activity of the Holy Spirit. Our role is to engage people in thoughtful and sometimes disruptive discussions. We are also to present the content of the gospel creatively.

Presenting the Gospel Creatively

As we have already seen, especially in the life of Christ himself, there are many different and creative ways of presenting the gospel.

René and I had worked together on a major research project. He was a gifted graphic artist. We were in his favorite restaurant having lunch together to celebrate the end of the venture when he made this announcement about his beliefs: "I don't believe in politicians or preachers. I don't believe in advertising. I believe in the natural laws of the universe. If I work hard and do good work, life will come my way."

"René, my friend," I explained, "there are other laws in this life that you need to know about, and you cannot escape them. Besides the physical laws like the law of gravity, there are societal laws like the criminal code. No matter what you believe, if you rob a bank and get caught, you will go to jail. There are also moral laws. For instance, selfishness is destructive. When selfishness rules, you are not fit to live with yourself or with others. And just like these other laws, there are also spiritual laws. God is Creator, Redeemer and Judge. Everyone sins and insults the Creator. Everyone can be redeemed in Christ. And no matter who you are or what you believe, everyone will be judged in the end."

There is little debate about the historical existence of Jesus. Even

Islam acknowledges and affirms his prophet-teacher status. Presenting the gospel around the different views people have of Jesus will be fruitful for the kingdom.

Many cultural Christians see Jesus as a *Teacher*—he is wise and has good ideas—and as a *Model*—his example is a pattern for right living. But these cultural views of Jesus reduce him to being no more than an impressive human being. C. S. Lewis rightly contends that cultural views of Jesus are not only incomplete, they are foolish. People often say: "I'm ready to accept Jesus as a great moral teacher, but I don't accept his claim to be God." Lewis reasons, "That is the one thing we must not say. A man who was merely a man and said the sort of things Jesus said would not be a great moral teacher. He would either be a lunatic—on a level with the man who says he is a poached egg—or else he would be the Devil of Hell. You must make your choice."[3]

To be consistent, Christians must go further and affirm Jesus as *Savior*—he died to redeem the world—and as *Lord*—he deserves to be obeyed. Christian views of Jesus affirm both his impressive humanity and his unequalled divinity. Jesus frequently asked his disciples to commit their loyalty to him and his mission. When Jesus was teaching and the crowds were rejecting him, Jesus turned to his disciples and gave them the option of leaving too. Simon Peter spoke with wisdom and conviction: "Lord, to whom shall we go? You have the words of eternal life. We believe and know that you are the Holy One of God" (Jn 6:69).

Some people are naturally more cognitively inclined. They may respond to a presentation of the gospel as a world view in contrast to other world views. Some current popular world views include the *human potential movement,* where people like Leo Buscaglia and others teach that humankind is basically good, that human ingenuity is life's best gift, that God is an optional extra, that self-discovery and self-respect are the goals of life; the *New Age movement,* where people like Shirley Maclaine and others teach that we are all gods, that we create our own reality, that altered states of consciousness help us grow and learn, that there is no real difference between good and evil, that we will be reincarnated and that we have control over our own destiny;[4] and the *Christian faith movement,* where Jesus and his disciples teach that God is Creator and Redeemer, that the Bible is the primary source of revelation, that Jesus came to earth to save the world from sin, that despite our sinfulness we are promised redemption from God through the forgiveness of sins, abundant life on earth and eternal life with God after death.

Whether people are able to consciously articulate it or not, everyone lives with a world view. Early church father Augustine astutely concluded that God "hath made us for [himself] and our hearts are restless until they find their rest in [him]." Since the beginning of time, the place God made for himself has either been given over to him or has been replaced by other understandings of life and alternative forms of worship.

In a culture that treasures relationships and values family, it is fruitful to present the gospel around the analogy that becoming and being a Christian is like falling in love and getting married.[5] First there is the *courtship stage* where you check out the potential for a relationship, form a friendship, chase away the doubts and fall in love with the Savior. Next is the *wedding day* where you make the commitment, declare the covenantal "I do," embrace your partner and celebrate with the family. Afterward comes *living in the marriage* where you grow in your relationship with Christ as Lord, live out the love affair, say no to other love affairs and add to God's family.

If we are open and willing, God will give us opportunities to imaginatively explain the gospel in ways that make sense to the people God brings into our lives.

The Urgency of the Gospel

Within the past year I was invited by a school board to address several high-school assemblies on the subject of self-worth. I was given a blank-check opportunity to bring an affirming address to thousands of students. In my presentation on the Parable of the Talents (Mt 21:33-46), I stressed the need for them to be careful in what they believed, because it would affect how they behaved.

During a question-and-answer period, one young woman, whom I would judge was in the twelfth grade, took the microphone and, in front of nine hundred fellow students, asked the question, "Are you disappointed that our generation doesn't believe in God very much?"

Although I made a faithful attempt, the question was more profound than my response. What I wish I had said is, "I'm even more than disappointed—I'm afraid for you. Do you realize it is dangerous to live without God?"

By contrast, a young woman I know has discovered the joy of living with Jesus. Karen met Christ in her early twenties and continues to go deep in her commitment to live the Christian life. She sums up her vibrant perspective:

"It's exciting to know that Christians can be the most whole people walking the face of the earth."

As followers of Jesus, we are privileged people. Our life in Christ not only launches us on a journey toward wholeness, our experiences in life fit with God's original design for his creation. Engaging the modern world around us with a credible gospel offers us another privilege. We have the delight of working with God to invite the people who touch our lives to join the journey too.

Postscript

Engaging the culture in order to present a credible gospel will require clear choices and deliberate strategies from today's Christians. Those who live with a faith commitment in Jesus and have a desire to share his mission can engage the culture with an approach that keeps several key principles in mind.

Resisting Assimilation

Christians will say no to the repeated invitation to conform to the world's patterns, and not become like the world. Rather than being seduced by the cultural norms, they will reach up to the standards of Christ. They will not be absorbed by the spirit of the age or be blown around by the winds of the latest trends. They will fight against thinking as the world thinks and living as the world lives. Instead, they will live out their beliefs in the midst of a society that believes other things about what is right and best and good.

Rejecting Abdication

The people of God who want to engage the culture will not retreat into Christian ghettos. They will deplore escaping from the world. Rather, they will become alarmed when their significant relationships do not include non-Christians. They will aim to keep their membership in good standing in both the church and the world. They will be regular participants in the life of the church, but they will also be alert to the danger of becoming permanent residents in a Christian subculture. They will be realistic about evil and the dangers of living in the world. They will go wherever God sends them. In fact, to disengage from the society in which they live would mark their lives with disobedience toward the Lord they love.

Giving Permission

Committed Christians in these times will remember that God gave them the choice to accept or reject his ways. They will treat the people in their lives like God treated them. They will give people permission to choose what to believe and how to behave. They will respect the God-given rights of those who are not Christian believers. They will be empathetic people. They will assume the posture of St. Francis and "seek to understand rather than just to be understood."

Accept People

As committed followers of Jesus they will accept people whether those people have accepted Jesus or not. They will understand that accepting people is neither agreeing with them nor approving of what they do. Rather, they will know that acceptance is an open-arms attitude that enables people to step toward each other.

Appreciate People

As serious Christians engaging the culture they will appreciate people for who they are. They will choose to value the people in their lives and know that everyone in the world has been touched with the goodness of God's creation. They will not reduce people to evangelistic projects or witness with a "hit and run" mentality. Mutual respect will enhance their relationships.

Influence People

Dedicated Christians wanting to be faithful will also live with an intentional commitment to influence people. They will assume that Christ's mission is their mission too. Like shifting a cart into gear so it can move ahead, engaging the culture evangelistically will invite interactions with people for the purpose of prompting them to move toward God.

Engaging to Transform

The people of God who engage the culture will interject God's transforming truth and the presence of Jesus into life situations. They will enjoy the people God brings into their lives. They will be dissatisfied with shallow relationships. Those who do not know God will be intrigued by their wholeness.

Pray and Experience God

There will be no confusion about who is the Creator and who are the created ones. They will know God personally. They will taste the joy of his personal presence. They will pray to edify their own relationship with their Heavenly Father, and they will intercede for the people who move in and out of their lives. They will watch God at work in their world, and their faith will be inspired by what they see.

Care for People and Themselves

For faithful Christians in today's world, word claims alone will be an inadequate definition of what a Christian is. Theoretical claims of belief will be demonstrated. Words will be spoken with caring deeds. People will be touched. Human pain will be reduced. Cups of water will be poured in the name of Christ, and people will be compelled to believe.

Communicate God's Truth

Letting Jesus be their model, today's Christians who engage the culture will interact with ideas. They will struggle to find God's point of view on matters of personal interest and on the broader issues of social concern. They will use words to complement their deeds. They will speak the truth and interpret the times. People around them will want to know what they think.

The people of God who pray and care and communicate will be people of hope. Spiritual energy will flow out of the reality of their life in Christ. They will not be surprised by frequent divine visits. In fact, they will expect their Heavenly Father to miraculously break into their circumstances. Every day will not be bright and beautiful, but the whole of life will resonate with harmonious design.

GOING FURTHER: EXERCISES FOR INDIVIDUALS AND GROUPS

Chapter 1: Leaving Our Safety Zones

1. Reflect
Name the people in your natural networks. Make a list of family and friends, people at work and school, and others with whom you share common interests. Identify at least three people on your list who would not claim to be serious Christians. Where do you think these individuals feel most comfortable? In other words, where are their comfort zones?

2. Read Luke 19:1-10.

3. Discuss
What facts do we know about Zacchaeus? Based on how Zacchaeus acted, what else can we surmise about him?

How did Jesus respond to Zacchaeus's initiative? How did the people who were present react to Jesus?

After Jesus left his comfort zone to enter Zacchaeus's world, Zacchaeus turned from his old ways and changed his behavior. Describe the changes in Zacchaeus's behavior.

In your thinking, what are some examples of distinctive behavior that should mark the lives of modern Christians? How does knowing Christ and following him affect your behavior?

Zacchaeus was drawn toward Jesus. In your view, what kinds of behavior from today's Christians will intrigue non-Christians enough to prompt them to investigate the faith for themselves?

What are your comfort zones, and what would it take for you to venture out of them? What would motivate you to enter other people's comfort zones?

4. Act

Pray: Express gratitude to God for the people who are a part of your world. Review the list of individuals in your natural networks. Ask God to give you a deeper friendship with one or two non-Christians you frequently see.

Care: Extending dignity to people is an act of care. Put yourself in the shoes of a door-to-door vacuum salesperson, for example. Salespeople experience repeated rejection. The next time one knocks on your door, treat that person with respect and put him or her at ease.

Take another look at the people in your natural networks. Identify one person on your list who you perceive is under some kind of pressure. Plan to spend some time with that person where he or she feels most comfortable. Express your awareness of his or her situation and your concern. Enjoy whatever happens.

Communicate: Talk with one or two people in your natural networks who are non-Christians. Tell them about your small-group discussion (exercise 3 above). Ask them for their impressions of Christians and how they think followers of Jesus should act in our kind of world.

Chapter 2: Becoming Meaning-Makers

1. Reflect
Think back to an occasion when God clearly answered a specific prayer on your behalf. What thoughts of God does that evoke in you?

Describe an instance when someone cared for you. What thoughts did you have about that person? Complete the statement, "When someone cares for me . . ."

Describe how you feel when someone is talking "at you" rather than interacting "with you." What thoughts do you have about the person? How do you know when someone is really listening to you? How does it make you feel?

2. Read Luke 10:25—11:13.

3. Discuss
Jesus assumes different gestures and uses distinctive styles to communicate in each of these four situations in Luke. Make a list of the principles of communication Jesus demonstrates. Why do you think the four instances are so different from each other?

What do you learn from Jesus' approach?

Make three or four statements to summarize the content of Jesus' teaching on caring for people in the parable of the good Samaritan (10:30-37).

Make three or four statements to summarize the content of Jesus' teaching on the subject of prayer (11:1-13).

Identify one or two of the communication principles Jesus practiced that you would like to implement. How can you implement these principles? Covenant with someone to follow through on your good intentions.

4. Act

Pray: Work your way through the Lord's Prayer phrase by phrase. Take time to let God's Spirit help you contemplate each phrase.

Care: Care for yourself. Go out and buy your favorite ice cream cone or some other favorite treat. Think about how God has gifted you. Thank God for creating you with the capacity to care for others.

Think about someone who is a shut-in or lives alone. Consider arranging to provide supper for that person within the next couple of weeks. Bring along flowers and stay around to wash the dishes.

Communicate: Recall the major steps that prompted you to commit your life to Christ. Think about the reasons that convince you to continue to follow Jesus. Get together with another Christian and share your stories with each other. Critique each other. Make your assessments on the basis of how non-Christians will understand your story. Then ask God to give you opportunities to tell your story to individuals who are not yet Christian believers.

Chapter 3: Overcoming Intimidation

1. Reflect
In your mind take a cultural walk through the primary environments where you spend most of your time (work, school, neighborhood, recreation, church and so on). What are the values, ethics, pleasures, problems and aspirations that dominate these worlds?

How are Christians and the church being overly influenced by what controls the world—or how are they exerting a strong Christian influence?

2. Read Numbers 13:1—14:9.

3. Discuss
Moses sent the spies out to "explore" the land of Canaan. What did Moses ask them to look for (13:16-20)? What did they find (13:26-29)?

The twelve spies brought back both a majority and a minority report. What reasons did the ten spies give to support their recommendation not to conquer the land (13:26-33)? What did Caleb and Joshua say to back their appeal to go and take the land (14:5-9)?

Which position do you think you would have supported? Why? (Be honest.) Are there specific circumstances in your world that intimidate you or make you feel like a grasshopper?

When do you feel strong in your land? What factors need to be in place for you to feel like you can influence people for God and good in your land? What do you learn from Caleb and Joshua?

What steps can we take to prepare ourselves for situations that threaten to silence our witness in this world?

4. Act

Pray: Thank God for his commitment to his people throughout history. Pray for a sense of God's presence and power as you walk in your land. Pray that God's people will resist the forces of secularization so persuasive in today's world. Pray for God's strength to resist the pressures of intimidation.

Care: Simply motivated by the value of getting to know someone new, ask a person you don't know very well out for lunch or a Coke and pick up the tab. Or break the silence with someone in pain. Telephone, write, go visit someone who is struggling—with a recent death in their family, the prospect of terminal illness, alienation from a son or daughter, a job demotion, a firing, or some other serious difficulty. Express your interest and desire to help. Then offer specific assistance.

Communicate: With someone in your land, initiate a conversation that deals with what influences you. Express concern about how the world shapes our values. Solicit the other person's view. Reflect on the kind of society we are creating for the next generation.

Chapter 4: Engaging Pluralism

1. Reflect

What are some of the stereotypes Christians have of non-Christians and non-Christians have of Christians? What impact do these stereotypes have on relationships between Christians and non-Christians?

How can the approach recommended in this chapter—to accept, appreciate and influence people—counteract the impact of stereotyping?

2. Read Acts 17:16-34.

3. Discuss

How did Paul respond to the city of Athens? What did he see? How did he react? What did he do (vv. 16-17)?

Assess your own society. Looking at the big picture, identify a few major aspects of our society that encourage you and a few aspects that concern and trouble you.

Paul perceived that the Athenians had different "objects of worship" (vv. 22-23). What are people around you worshiping today? What powers control people's behavior in this age?

In order to make the "unknown God" known, Paul listed several of God's characteristics (vv. 24-31). Make a list of the characteristics Paul ascribes to God. Among the characteristics Paul mentions, which ones do you appreciate most? Why?

Think about a friend or member of your family who has not accepted Christ at this stage in his or her life. Which characteristics about

God do you think would be attractive to him or her? What response is this person making to Christ? Why do you believe he or she is responding that way? Initiate a conversation within the next week with this person to see if your impressions are accurate. Ask the person why he or she has concluded that God is not ultimately important. Listen.

4. Act

Pray: Thank God for his decision to give us choices. Pray that we will have good judgment in the choices we make. Pray particularly for people close to you who have not yet decided to accept Christ that they will give him the place he deserves in their lives.

Care: Move toward a lifestyle that sees needs and responds. Console a lost child in a department store. Stop on the highway and help change a flat tire. When the kids in your neighborhood set up a lemonade stand, buy a drink and talk for a little while. Chase after someone who has inadvertently dropped something. Buy a meal for someone begging on the street. Give up your place in line at the grocery store for someone who is obviously in a hurry.

Communicate: Make an "I believe" statement this week to someone you see frequently. For example, "I believe our society is giving us too many choices," or, "I believe we have become too tolerant in this age." Look for opportunities to speak definitively but appropriately. Offer your point of view in such a way that it stimulates a conversation. Ask that person what he or she believes about the subject.

Chapter 5: Decoding Cultural Christianity

1. Reflect

Compile a list of the values and virtues that are generally accepted to be good and right in today's society (for example, honesty and for-giveness). Assess how many of them are directly linked to Christian teaching.

Compile another list noting both the cultural/religious events in a calendar year and the kinds of public ceremonies that include some expression of what is specifically religious (for example, prayer and the Bible). What are some other examples of the cultural/religious blend in today's society?

2. Read Mark 6:1-6.

3. Discuss

Just prior to returning home in Nazareth, Jesus had performed what must be considered the ultimate miracle. He raised a little girl from the dead. Whatever his hometown friends had heard about his public ministry, Jesus had enough credibility in their eyes to be the guest sabbath teacher at the synagogue. How did the audience respond to Jesus' teaching? How did the debate polarize around him?

Based on the information in the text, if the members of the crowd were polled that morning, how would they have responded to the question: "Who do you think Jesus is?"

In the end, how did the crowd respond to Jesus (vv. 3, 6)? Why did Jesus became somewhat exasperated with the crowd (v. 4)?

Because of our cultural inheritance, Jesus' name and face are familiar in today's society. What are some ways we may incite some constructive debate about Jesus?

How can we bring freshness to things people have heard about before? How are preconceived impressions altered in this world? What factors have prompted you to change your mind about some issues or ideas?

Make some suggestions that may prod people to move from a state of just being familiar with Jesus to making a personal commitment to him.

4. Act

Pray: Pray for the people in our society who make decisions that have a direct impact on others—government leaders, business executives, educators, doctors, labor leaders, judges and others who come to mind—that they will be principled and compassionate, good trustees of their responsibilities, and that they will not think of themselves more highly than they ought.

Care: In today's world, unless a generous gratuity is left behind, praying before a meal can be a negative witness. The next time you go out for lunch, particularly on a Sunday, even if the service is just ordinary, leave an extraordinary tip.

Praying is an expression of care. Write a note to someone for whom you have recently prayed. Inquire about their well-being and offer your interest and concern.

Communicate: Get together with someone you enjoy and appreciate who is not a Christian. Tell them you recently read a book that pointed out that eight out of ten people in North America claim to believe that Jesus is the divine Son of God. Ask the person what he or she believes about Jesus. Relax and enjoy the discussion.

Chapter 6: Embracing God's Diversity

1. Reflect

Consider the statement: "Whether we are dealing with alternative ways of being Christian or with other world religions, our approach must be marked with modesty and respect." Do you agree or disagree? Why?

Why should we respect the views of others? What produces genuine modesty in us?

2. Read 1 Corinthians 1:1-12.

3. Discuss

Why is Paul thankful for the Corinthian Christians? How does he specifically compliment and affirm them?

Describe the problem Paul is addressing. What does he ask the Corinthians to do to resolve the problem?

Later in the letter Paul claims that one of the reasons for divisions in the church was because the Corinthian Christians were "unspiritual," "worldly" and "mere infants in Christ" (3:1). How do you think these contribute to divisions in the church? In what ways do you think modern divisions in the church are similarly caused?

Even though Paul was aware of serious problems inside the Corinthian church, he was able to affirm the people in the situation. Identify a church denomination or tradition far different from your own. Make a list of its strengths—the "treasures" it contributes to God's great kingdom. Make another list identifying what you consider to be the strengths of your church. Compare the two lists. How do they affect your view of both?

How can we resolve the tension of both appreciating other points of view while still maintaining a strong commitment to our own?

4. Act

Pray: Thank God for his gift of diversity in the world. Praise him for all the treasures you have received from all the different church traditions in history.

Care: Think about someone with whom you have frequent contact who looks at life much differently than you. Make an extra effort to understand that person. Look for a situation to give that person a genuine compliment.

Communicate: Enter into a conversation with another Christian from a different church tradition from your own or preferably with a person who embraces one of the world's other religions. Discuss the issues involved in appreciating what other people believe while at the same time retaining a strong commitment to your own beliefs. If the situation is appropriate, explore what the other person thinks about the model of accepting, appreciating and influencing people.

Chapter 7: Personalizing Our Witness

1. *Reflect*

Think back to your spiritual pilgrimage. Remember the individuals who influenced you. What is unique about your experience? Share your story with the group.

Recognizing how God dealt differently with you from others in your group, what can we expect from God when it comes to how he will deal with people who have not yet come to faith? How should God's approach to dealing with people affect how we communicate the truth of the gospel to the people around us?

2. *Read* John 20:25-29.

3. *Discuss*

What evidence is there in the text to indicate that Jesus really knew and understood Thomas?

What does this incident tell us about Thomas's temperament? How did Jesus' manner of dealing with Thomas fit this temperament? What principles seem to guide Jesus' style of interacting with people?

Jesus treated everyone who came to him in a unique way. What will it take for us to relate to people and witness to them in this way?

Jesus was candid with people but he also freed people to reveal their true selves. What did Jesus signal to people that allowed them to be vulnerable? How can we be like him?

Thomas struggled with doubt. Do you know some people who are like Thomas? How do you think they would answer the question,

"What would it take for you to believe in Jesus?"

What are some of the obstacles today that stand in the way of people believing in Jesus and following him? How can they be removed?

4. Act

Pray: Think of one non-Christian whom you interact with regularly. Spend twenty minutes in prayer for him or her, thanking God for their particular gifts and for how they enrich your life, praying for all their needs, goals and wishes, and for how you will be able to reach out to them in a specific, personal way.

Care: Sometimes it is easier to care for people at work or those who live next door than it is to say, "I'm sorry" or "I love you" to members of your immediate family. Think about your mother or father, sister or brother, son or daughter, spouse or another who is close to you. If it is possible, go and tell them how much you appreciate them. If a personal contact is not feasible, do it in writing or with a phone call.

Communicate: What do you think God is saying to some of the non-Christians in your life? Think about one or two of these people with whom you have significant relationships. Pray that God's Spirit will awaken them to his desires for them. Expect God to act. Take initiative in their direction. Tell them that you have been praying for them.

Chapter 8: Using Our Minds

1. Reflect
Review the front-page stories from this past week's newspapers. Identify at least five separate issues and areas of concern—whether they be political, economic, social problems, family issues, medical concerns, ethical dilemmas, international catastrophes or other matters. Using your Christian mind, discuss what could be God's point of view on what is going on in our world. What do you think God thinks about these matters?

2. Read Colossians 2:6-8.

3. Discuss
Verse 6 distinguishes between "receiving Christ" and "living in him." How do the two ideas relate to each other?

What are some practical ways to be "rooted, built up and strengthened" in Christ?

Paraphrase verse 8 and share your version with the group.

Our culture often conflicts with the teachings and wishes of Christ for his people. Assess the following statements and ponder the philosophies of life they endorse: "I'll do it my way." "It's all relative." "Eat, drink and be merry." "Clothes make the man." "Look out for number one." "Don't make waves." "Science is the answer." "God is a crutch." To which of these suggestions from the world are you especially vulnerable?

As followers of Jesus in today's world, how can we help each other resist the temptations of the times? How can we encourage each other to live a life of joyful obedience?

4. Act

Pray: With a newspaper in front of you, pray for the people and concerns in the different stories. Take a globe or map of the world and pray around the world. Focus on countries where there is political unrest and oppression, war, racial tension, poverty and hunger. Pray that justice will prevail. Pray that Christians who live in those lands will be wise and brave. Pray that the United Nations and other human structures will be instruments of peace and equality in today's world.

Care: Do a needs assessment of your own community. Go to your local park early in the morning and pick up litter. If unemployment is high, attempt to find at least one job for someone you know. If you are a student in a campus residence, turn your room into a hospitality center by popping popcorn once a week, pouring a few free Cokes and cultivating your listening skills. Or if you work, plan to get there a little early. Take a few moments to observe your colleagues as they arrive. Look below the surface of their lives. Ask the Holy Spirit to give you insight about them. Make mental notes about how you might appropriately affirm two or three of your fellow workers in the next few days.

Communicate: Continue to monitor the events and concerns that surface in the daily newspaper. Study both the implicit and explicit messages harbored in advertisements. When a concern or issue grips your mind and heart, or when an advertisement crosses the line and offends you, take initiative to discuss what you think with someone who is not yet a Christian. Ask them what they think. Include the statement, "As a Christian, I'm troubled because . . ."

Chapter 9: Transcending Words

1. Reflect
Recall an instance when someone cared for you. How did you feel when someone took the time to care for your needs? Describe how you felt toward that individual. Take a moment and pray with thanksgiving for that person.

2. Read Matthew 5:43-47 and Mark 10:42-45.

3. Discuss
In Matthew 5:43-47 what standard does Jesus set for his followers? How are they to be distinct from non-Christians?

In Mark 10, James and John are striving for advancement and position in the kingdom. When Jesus said to his disciples, "Not so with you," how was he asking them to be different?

Being a servant has very little status in society. What will it take to resist the pervasive influence of the world at this point and live according to Jesus' standard?

What will be the consequences of ignoring Jesus' standards and surrendering to the world's ways?

Identify a particular person in a situation who has real needs that you can serve. Covenant with someone that you are going to act.

Purpose to serve people and care more. Identify someone in your life who is shy or somewhat withdrawn. Make an effort to include that person in an activity with you and attempt to introduce him or her to one of your friends. Offer to take care of your neighbor's apartment or house while they are on vacation. Invite someone into your home who is not likely to invite you back in return. Consider serving as a volunteer. Read to the blind, work at a food bank, join a hospital auxiliary, teach someone how to read, drive people to medical appointments. When you arrive at the tennis court about the same time as other players, offer the first available court to them—with a smile. Lift the level of life around you!

4. Act

Pray: Ask God to reveal to you specific ways you can act in a more distinctively Christian manner.

Go for a walk on a busy street. In the midst of the traffic and diesel fumes from buses and trucks, with people smoking and swearing around you, note the litter and garbage that people have left behind, study the environment, look at the expressions on people's faces, and as you walk along, pray. Let the activity around you channel your thoughts and stimulate prayers of petition and praise.

Care: Think of some skill or expertise that you have that would be of benefit to someone else and volunteer your services.

Identify a single parent you know. The person may be from your work world, your church, or live down the street or across the hall. Offer to babysit the children for an evening. Place a twenty-dollar bill in a humorous card to help with the celebration.

Think about someone who would benefit from learning something you know. Offer to help. It may be tutoring a fellow student, assisting someone in the office who is struggling with a computer software program, working with a neighbor who is a novice carpenter or helping your son or daughter with a project.

Communicate: Think back to a recent situation where you acted in a manner that was not becoming to a Christian. If Jesus had been present he might have said, "Not so with you." Consider going to the person involved, confessing your concern and asking for forgiveness.

Chapter 10: Helping People Decide

1. Reflect
Using language that would not normally be considered as religious, develop a list of synonyms and expressions that convey the biblical meaning of "being born again" and "being reconciled with God." Use analogies or metaphors. Complete the statement, "To me, becoming a Christian is like . . ."

Again without using religious language, share the meaning of "salvation" with another Christian as though you were talking with a non-Christian friend.

2. Read Acts 26:15-18.

3. Discuss
In his defense before King Agrippa, Paul seized the opportunity to share his own story of how Christ confronted and redeemed him on the road to Damascus. What three images did Jesus give Paul to describe how he was to help the Gentiles come to God?

When people "open their eyes" and come to God, what do they receive?

What role do seasoned Christians have in consolidating the faith of new believers?

Paul had a clear sense of being "sent" to the Gentiles. Has God given you a special sense of mission for a specific situation or group of people? If not, where and with whom do you think God would like you to make his ways known?

Opening blind eyes, turning people from darkness to light and from the power of Satan to the power of God is not a task God has put solely in human hands. How do we complement what God's Spirit is doing? What is the human role in helping people come to God?

Since turning to God normally happens over an extended period of time, how can we communicate the claims of the gospel so that people do not turn away before they have given God serious consideration?

What forces and factors discourage us from expressing our human responsibility in evangelism?

4. Act

Pray: Go some place where you will not be interrupted and take some extra time to be alone with God. Ask God to make himself known to you in a fresh way. Pray especially that he would pour the strength of his character into yours so that you can live with integrity in today's world. Ask God for his joy to uplift others around you, for his love to reach out and touch others, for his truth to reveal his ways and for his power to overcome evil with good.

Care: Practice the grace principle this week. Extend the right to fail to someone in your life by accepting their incompleteness or immaturity. In another relationship, care enough to correct. Offer a constructive criticism to someone with whom you have strong rapport.

Convene a family conference. Review the family's commitment to give to charitable causes. Determine your giving priorities for the next six months. If possible, give your children the prerogative to designate a gift. Give them suggestions if needed. Decide to send an encouragement gift to someone for which you will not receive a receipt for tax purposes.

Communicate: What is your way to present the content of the gospel? Be prepared. Develop a plan or a number of plans of salvation that make sense to you. Construct them in a manner that will free you to share them with a non-Christian friend or contact. Pray that God will open the way for you to present the gospel to someone within the next month.

Notes

Chapter 1: Leaving Our Comfort Zones

[1]Peter Berger, *The Heretical Imperative* (Garden City, N.Y.: Anchor Press, 1979), pp. 16-17.

[2]Charles Colson, *Presenting Belief in an Age of Unbelief* (Wheaton, Ill.: Victor Books, 1986), pp. 5-6.

[3]George Gallup, Jr., "Secularism and Religion: Trends in Contemporary America," *Emerging Trends* 9 (December 1987), 10:3.

[4]Dean Borgman, "Faculty Letter to Our Alumni," Gordon Conwell Seminary, May 1988.

[5]Reginald Bibby, *Fragmented Gods* (Toronto: Irwin, 1987), pp. 211-13.

[6]Norval Geldenhuys, *Commentary on the Gospel of Luke*, The New International Commentary on the New Testament (Grand Rapids, Mich.: Eerdmans, 1951), p. 470.

[7]George MacDonald, *Getting to Know Jesus* (New Canaan, Conn.: Keats Publishing, 1980), p. 145.

[8]Quoted in Gallup, "Secularism and Religion."

[9]Quoted by James Reichley, *Religion in American Public Life* (Washington, D.C.: Brookings Institution, 1985), p. 360.

[10]Ibid., p. 359.

[11]John Stott, *Christian Mission in the Modern World* (Downers Grove, Ill.: InterVarsity Press, 1975), p. 32.

200 REINVENTING EVANGELISM

Chapter 2: Becoming Meaning-Makers

[1]Lesslie Newbigin, *Foolishness to the Greeks* (Grand Rapids, Mich.: Eerdmans, 1986), p. 20.

[2]William Barclay, *The Plain Man Looks at the Lord's Prayer* (London: Collins, 1964), p. 54.

[3]C. S. Lewis, *The Business of Heaven* (London: Collins, 1984), p. 17.

[4]Allan Bloom, *The Closing of the American Mind* (New York: Simon and Schuster, 1987), p. 25.

[5]Ibid., pp. 25, 28.

[6]Dorothy Sayers, *A Matter of Eternity* (Grand Rapids, Mich.: Eerdmans, 1973), pp. 16-17.

Chapter 3: Overcoming Intimidation

[1]William Diehl, *In Search of Faithfulness* (Philadelphia: Fortress, 1987), p. 7.

[2]Douglas Webster, *A Passion for Christ* (Grand Rapids, Mich.: Academie/ Zondervan, 1987), p. 13.

[3]Neil Postman, *Amusing Ourselves to Death* (New York: Penguin Books, 1985), pp. 1-3.

[4]J. Russell Hale, *The Unchurched: Who They Are and Why They Stay Away* (New York: Harper & Row, 1980), p. 47.

[5]Glenn Smith, as quoted in *Christian Week*, 13 Sept. 1988.

[6]Hale, *Unchurched*, p. 107.

[7]James Engel, as cited in "Evangelism, Secularization and the Navigators" (Wheaton, Ill.: Management Development Associates, January 1987), a report by the Eastern Division Steering committee on Secularization in the U.S.A.

[8]Statistics drawn from Gallup Poll 1985.

[9]Reginald Bibby, *Fragmented Gods* (Toronto: Irwin Publishing, 1987). The data for this section was collected from pages 17, 93 and 99.

Chapter 4: Engaging Pluralism

[1]Newbigin, *Foolishness to the Greeks*, p. 17.

[2]Bloom, *Closing of the American Mind*, p. 27.

[3]John Stott, *Involvement: Being a Responsible Christian in a Non-Christian Society*, vol. 1 (Old Tappan, N.J.: Revell, 1984), p. 75.

[4]Ajith Fernando, *The Christian's Attitude toward World Religions* (Wheaton, Ill.: Tyndale, 1987), p. 26.

[5]Jay Newman, *Foundations of Religious Tolerance* (Toronto: University of Toronto Press, 1982), p. 105.

[6]M. Scott Peck, *The Different Drum* (New York: Simon and Schuster, 1987), p. 20.

[7]F. F. Bruce, *The Acts of the Apostles* (Grand Rapids, Mich.: Eerdmans, 1952), p. 242.

[8]Fernando, *Christian's Attitude toward World Religions,* p. 93.

Chapter 5: Decoding Cultural Christianity
[1]Don Posterski and Reginald Bibby, *Canada's Youth: Ready for Today* (Ottawa: Government of Canada, 1988), pp. 47-48.
[2]High levels of religious identity also exist in the United States. Even 82% of the unchurched cite a religious affiliation ("The Unchurched American—10 Years Later," a pamphlet of The Princeton Religion Research Center, 1988).
[3]Ninety-six per cent of Canadians affirm honesty as a "very important" value (Bibby, *Fragmented Gods,* p. 168).
[4]Don Posterski, *Friendship: A Window on Ministry to Youth* (Scarborough: Project Teen America, 1985), p. 33.
[5]Sean O'Sullivan, *Both My Houses* (Toronto: Key Porter Books, 1986), p. 235.
[6]Frederick Buechner, *The Magnificent Defeat* (New York: Seabury, 1966), p. 110.

Chapter 6: Embracing God's Diversity
[1]*Toronto Star,* April 2, 1987.
[2]Richard John Neuhaus, *The Naked Public Square* (Grand Rapids, Mich.: Eerdmans, 1984), p. 21.
[3]Peter Wagner, *Effective Body Building* (San Bernardino, Calif.: Here's Life, 1982), pp. 41-56.
[4]The idea was part of a verbal conversation and attributed to Kilian McDonnel, a monk at St. John's Abbey in Collegeville, Minnesota.
[5]Neuhaus, *Naked Public Square,* p. 17.
[6]Interview with Peter Mason in *Christian Week* (a newspaper published in Winnipeg, Manitoba), July 21, 1987.

Chapter 7: Personalizing Our Witness
[1]Malcolm Muggeridge, *Something Beautiful for God* (Garden City, N.Y.: Image/Doubleday, 1971).
[2]Posterski and Bibby, *Canada's Youth,* pp. 8, 10.
[3]Bibby, *Fragmented Gods,* p. 167.
[4]John Naisbitt, *Megatrends* (New York: Warner, 1982), p. 53.
[5]David Lyon, *The Silicon Society* (Grand Rapids, Mich.: Eerdmans, 1986), p. 19.
[6]John MacArthur, *The Gospel According to Jesus* (Grand Rapids, Mich.: Zondervan, 1988), p. 37.
[7]Don Posterski, *Why Am I Afraid to Tell You I'm a Christian?* (Downers Grove, Ill.: InterVarsity Press, 1983), p. 17.

[8]Arianna Huffington, *Toronto Life Fashion,* Fall 1988, p. 52.
[9]*Toronto Star,* September 18, 1988.

Chapter 8: Using Our Minds

[1]Lawrence Crabb, *Understanding People* (Grand Rapids, Mich.: Zondervan, 1987), p. 111.
[2]Bernard Ramm, *After Fundamentalism* (San Francisco: Harper & Row, 1983), pp. 66-67.
[3]C. S. Lewis, *Mere Christianity* (London: Collins, 1971), p. 165.
[4]A. S. Peake, *The Expositor's Greek New Testament,* vol. 1 (New York: Doran), p. 521.
[5]Frederick Buechner, *A Room Called Remember* (New York: Harper & Row, 1984), pp. 14-15.
[6]Lewis, *Mere Christianity,* p. 57.
[7]Harry Blamires, *The Christian Mind* (London: SPCK, 1963), especially see p. 43.
[8]Arthur Holmes, *All Truth Is God's Truth* (Downers Grove, Ill.: InterVarsity Press, 1977), p. 4.

Chapter 9: Transcending Words

[1]Alexander Astin, et al., *The American Freshman: Twenty Year Trends* (Los Angeles: University of California, 1987), p. 23.
[2]Posterski and Bibby, *Canada's Youth,* p. 21.
[3]Lewis, *Mere Christianity,* p. 172.
[4]Robert Greenleaf, *Servant Leadership* (New York: Paulist Press, 1977), pp. 13-14.
[5]Delos Miles, *Evangelism and Social Involvement* (Nashville: Broadman, 1986), p. 158.
[6]Frank Tillapaugh, *Unleashing Your Potential* (Ventura, Calif.: Regal, 1988), pp. 44-45.
[7]Ray Bakke, *The Urban Christian* (Downers Grove, Ill.: InterVarsity Press, 1987), p. 134.

Chapter 10: Helping People Decide

[1]Richard Niebuhr, *Christ and Culture* (New York: Harper & Row, 1951), pp. 39-44.
[2]Doug Stevens, *Called to Care* (Grand Rapids, Mich.: Zondervan, 1985), p. 95.
[3]Lewis, *Mere Christianity,* p. 52.
[4]James W. Sire, *The Universe Next Door* (Downers Grove, Ill.: InterVarsity Press, 1988), pp. 156-208.
[5]Posterski, *Why Am I Afraid?* p. 70.